Well-being and Growth in Advanced Economies

Economic growth is generally regarded by governments and most ordinary people as a panacea for all problems, including issues caused by the COVID pandemic. But this raises an important question: is further growth in advanced economies able to increase well-being once people's basic subsistence needs are met? Some advanced market economies, e.g., the United States, have exhibited a decline in well-being, both subjectively and objectively measured, over several decades despite seeing economic growth during the same period.

This book provides an original and comprehensive explanation: economic growth, as driven by market forces, induces people, through both the demand- and supply-side channels, to pursue command over more material resources, and this weakens the self-generation of capabilities, putting well-being at risk of deterioration. The book argues, with the support of a variety of evidence, that the challenge can be overcome if governments' policies and people's choices pursue, as their ultimate goal, 'fundamental human development' on an evolutionary basis: the development of the capability of a typical person to conceive and share with others new purposes, to pursue them individually or collectively, and thus to contribute to building human culture. If such human development is prioritised, it makes people satisfied with their lives and resistant to adverse shocks, and it can even shape the pattern of economic growth. By contrast, if economic growth is prioritised, it tends to weaken and impoverish fundamental human development and consequently people's well-being and social cohesion.

With this volume, readers will find an answer to a problem that is both urgent and long term, both individual and societal. The work makes a substantial contribution to the literature on well-being, the economics of happiness, human capital and growth, and the capability approach.

Maurizio Pugno (M.Phil., Cambridge, UK) is a full professor of economics at the University of Cassino, Italy.

Routledge Focus on Economics and Finance

The fields of economics are constantly expanding and evolving. This growth presents challenges for readers trying to keep up with the latest important insights. Routledge Focus on Economics and Finance presents short books on the latest big topics, linking in with the most cutting-edge economics research.

Individually, each title in the series provides coverage of a key academic topic, whilst collectively the series forms a comprehensive collection across the whole spectrum of economics.

Economics, Education and Youth Entrepreneurship
International Perspectives
Marian Noga and Andrzej Brzeziński

Markets vs Public Health Systems
Perspectives from the Austrian School of Economics
Łukasz Jasiński

Public Policy and the Impact of COVID-19 in Europe
Economic, Political and Social Dimensions
Magdalena Tomala, Maryana Prokop and Aleksandra Kordonska

Economic Innovations
Creating New Instruments to Improve Economic Life
Beth Webster and Bill Scales

Well-being and Growth in Advanced Economies
The Need to Prioritise Human Development
Maurizio Pugno

For more information about this series, please visit: www.routledge.com/ Routledge-Focus-on-Economics-and-Finance/book-series/RFEF

Well-being and Growth in Advanced Economies

The Need to Prioritise Human Development

Maurizio Pugno

LONDON AND NEW YORK

First published 2023
by Routledge
4 Park Square, Milton Park, Abingdon, Oxon OX14 4RN

and by Routledge
605 Third Avenue, New York, NY 10158

Routledge is an imprint of the Taylor & Francis Group, an informa business

© 2023 Maurizio Pugno

British Library Cataloguing-in-Publication Data

A catalogue record for this book is available from the British Library

Library of Congress Cataloging-in-Publication Data
Names: Pugno, Maurizio, author.
Title: Well-being and growth in advanced economies : the need to
   prioritise human development / Maurizio Pugno.
Description: Abingdon, Oxon ; New York, NY : Routledge, 2023. |
   Series: Routledge focus on economics and finance | Includes
   bibliographical references and index.
Identifiers: LCCN 2022019545 (print) | LCCN 2022019546 (ebook) |
   ISBN 9781032149059 (hardback) | ISBN 9781032149073 (paperback) |
   ISBN 9781003241676 (ebook)
Subjects: LCSH: Economic development—Social aspects—Developed
   countries. | Well-being—Developed countries. | Quality of life—
   Developed countries. | Social indicators—Developed countries.
Classification: LCC HD75 .P84 2023 (print) | LCC HD75 (ebook) |
   DDC 338.9—dc23/eng/20220421
LC record available at https://lccn.loc.gov/2022019545
LC ebook record available at https://lccn.loc.gov/2022019546

ISBN: 978-1-032-14905-9 (hbk)
ISBN: 978-1-032-14907-3 (pbk)
ISBN: 978-1-003-24167-6 (ebk)

DOI: 10.4324/9781003241676

Typeset in Times New Roman
by Apex CoVantage, LLC

To Irene
and to her lovable joy

Contents

About the author   ix

Acknowledgments   x

Introduction and summary   1

Prologue   5

1 Economic growth and people's well-being in advanced countries   7

  1.1 Economic growth and unsuccessful growth policies in advanced countries 7

  1.2 Does economic growth predict people's well-being in the advanced countries? 11

  1.3 The decline of well-being in the United States 15

  1.4 Economic growth and the deterioration of social cohesion 18

  Notes 21

  References 23

2 Human development and well-being   28

  2.1 In search of a human development that ensures well-being 28

  2.2 Human development as an expansion of the fundamental human capability 32

  2.3 The fundamental human capability in both human evolution and infancy 35

  2.4 Human development as a self-generating process 38

2.5 The path from human development to well-being 41
2.6 Ill-beings from weak human development 43
Notes 46
References 48

3   Why growth in market economies can deteriorate human development and well-being   55

3.1 A new and comprehensive explanation 55
3.2 Adverse shocks on the labour market and on workers' well-being 62
3.3 Education under market pressure 65
3.4 Parenting and children's development under market pressure 68
3.5 Addiction as self-medication 72
Notes 76
References 78

4   Economic growth and human development: which priority in the post-pandemic era?   87

4.1 The COVID-19 pandemic: hindrance or opportunity for human development? 87
4.2 Prioritising human development: how to relax its constrains 91
4.3 Prioritising human development: how to directly promote it 93
4.4 Prioritising human development: how to defend it 96
4.5 How human development can change the pattern of economic growth 99
Notes 102
References 104

Epilogue   110

Index   112

About the author

Maurizio Pugno (M.Phil., Cambridge, UK) is a full professor of economics at the University of Cassino, Italy. His publications are on economic growth, happiness, human and social capital, and economic psychology. He wrote a book on Roy Harrod in Italian, he co-edited the books *Productivity Growth and Economic Performance* (McMillan) and *Capabilities and Happiness* (Oxford University Press), and he recently published *On the Foundations of Happiness in Economics* (Routledge). He is a member of the World Well-Being Panel (an international panel of experts on well-being).

Acknowledgments

This book merges in relatively few pages four lines of research that I have done over the past three decades. The ideas that readers can find in the book have been discussed with so many people (and in so many places) that they cannot all be explicitly acknowledged. The four lines of research concern four topics: economic growth, well-being, human capabilities, and human capital. On economic growth, I can recall the 2002 book that I co-edited, *Productivity Growth and Economic Performance* (MacMillan). On well-being and human capabilities, I recently wrote *On the Foundations of Happiness in Economics* (Routledge) and co-edited in 2008 *Capabilities and Happiness* (Oxford University Press). Human capital is the central topic of a course that I have been teaching for 13 years. In merging these strands of research, not only economists but also psychologists influenced me, and when I had the opportunity of discussing with them, they also encouraged me. Among economists, I owe a great deal to Tibor Scitovsky and Richard Easterlin on well-being and economic growth, to Amartya Sen on human capabilities, and to James Heckman on human capital and capabilities. Among psychologists, I owe a lot to Mihaly Csikszentmihalyi and Richard Ryan on well-being. My acknowledgments should also go to the discussants at workshops and conferences, where I presented preparatory papers for the book, such as the Storep conference in Paris (2016), the A World to Win conference in Rotterdam (2017), the seminar in Statec (Luxembourg 2018), and the invited speech to the Einaudi Foundation (Turin 2019). I am further indebted to Francesco Farina, who carefully commented on the book, and to Paolo Conci, who has often forced me to clarify my writing. Finally, I acknowledge my department and university for the financial support and sabbatical leave granted to me for the preparatory research. A special grateful memory goes to Massimo Fagioli, without whom this book would not have been conceived.

Introduction and summary

The progress that has brought wealth to advanced countries has recurrently run into severe global crises. People wanted to go back to normal times, and governments reacted to revive the economy and bring it back to the old growth path. But the crises have also given voice to broader and longer-run complaints, which normally remain latent in good times.

In 1929, the deepest crisis of that century broke out, turning the impetuous economic growth of the Western world into widespread misery. Nevertheless, John M. Keynes, in one of his famous speeches, looked beyond the contingent concerns and wondered how the most advanced countries would grow from then to 100 years later and whether that economic growth would finally bring more happiness or not.

Almost a century later, a no less shocking crisis erupted due to the deadly COVID-19 pandemic, to breaks in productive activities, and to severe restrictions for millions of people. Everyone desired to return quickly to normality, but questions of a broader concern also emerged. "Are we happy with the progress we were building?", "Why weren't we prepared to face the pandemic?", and "Where will we go once the pandemic is over?"

Advances in our times cannot be ignored. Science and technology, together with massive economic resources, have provided us with countless and fantastic goods: from screen devices in our pockets and on desks to COVID-19 vaccines produced in a few months. However, we cannot ignore that, before the pandemic, the labour problems left by the 2008–2009 Great Recession had not yet been overcome, that the pandemic has exacerbated pre-existing dramatic inequalities and social divides, and that maintaining the old pattern of economic growth will certainly lead us to environmental catastrophe.

Several proposals are emerging to make economic growth more able to address social and environmental problems, thus giving people a happier future. A well-known approach proposes to focus on human capabilities not less than on the multiplication of material resources. Various lists of capabilities have thus been drawn up, followed by other lists of things to

DOI: 10.4324/9781003241676-1

capture what matters in the quality of life beyond mere gross domestic product (GDP). Another approach has recently become popular by recognising people's happiness as the final human goal, thus discovering that the contribution of income to subjective well-being is small albeit essential. Still others argue that greater social cooperation and a less hectic life should accompany environmentally sustainable economic growth.

This book builds on such proposals that move 'beyond GDP' to attack a broad and long-run problem that is becoming increasingly evident and urgent, at least in advanced countries. Namely, people do not seem to appreciate improvements in economic conditions and technological advances so much that they necessarily become more satisfied with their lives. Malaise is even spreading in countries that nevertheless exhibit economic growth. More generally, *although economic growth is able to solve the 'economic problem' by ensuring resources for subsistence, it can lead to a 'well-being problem' by failing to ensure people's necessary capability to enjoy their lives.*

The key problem addressed in the book, therefore, lies in the disappointing link going from economic growth to people's well-being in countries where subsistence needs are best met. The solution of the problem will be sought in people's capability to enjoy their lives. In fact – so the argument of the book will run – when economic growth is primarily driven by market forces, it changes people's *human development* as a side effect, which, in the long run, may become a deterioration, with negative consequences for well-being.

The concept of 'human development' is a central novelty of the book because it is based on the composite human capability which is most fundamental in human evolution and which has thus the properties of making development as self-generating and well-being as more resilient. These powerful properties suggest prioritising human development in people's choices and governments' policies, while economic growth should be a simple means to pursue it. In this way, the interpretation of the past can be combined with the prescriptions for a better future, and the other approaches of the movement going beyond GDP could be re-read from a different perspective and organised in a unitary framework.

Evidence, definitions, explanations, and recommendations find their place in the book as follows: the Prologue illustrates our key problem in the form of a prediction made many decades ago; the first chapter reports evidence showing the severity of the problem; the second chapter describes in some detail the new concept of human development; the third chapter adopts this concept to explain why the problem has arisen; the fourth chapter suggests prioritising human development as a way out from the problem; and finally, the Epilogue gives a representation of the urgency of taking up such priority.

A summary of the book can thus be arranged accordingly.

The key problem is raised in the Prologue by taking Keynes as a distinguished speaker. Indeed, in his 1930 speech, he not only argued that economic growth could solve the problem of finding what is needed to survive, but he also made a prediction which has been often neglected: that economic growth will not ensure well-being, but it can rather bring ill-beings. As Keynes vividly showed, the former is an 'economic problem' that humans share with other living beings, while the latter is a 'well-being problem' that is typically human and that we should prepare to solve.

Chapter 1 shows that economic growth in the past decades is far from ensuring improvements in people's well-being in the advanced countries. Since this result may be surprising, the chapter supports it by drawing various evidence from the literature, thus specifying four arguments. First, the trend of economic growth has substantially decelerated as countries have become affluent, despite different policies attempted to revive growth by relying on market forces. Second, the economic growth trend is unable to predict the trend of people's subjective well-being in the sample of advanced countries. Third, the most powerful market economy in the world, namely the United States, exhibits a tendential *decline* of well-being, variously measured, in the same past four decades in which it has grown by a multiple. Fourth, after governments' failures to revive growth, social cohesion, which is a collective measure of well-being, has seriously deteriorated in recent times.

The problem predicted by Keynes almost a century ago and then ascertained in our times requires identifying in people's lives the priority that ensures well-being once economic growth has solved the problem of satisfying their basic needs. But people's desires when affluence prevails are many and fickle and do not always ensure well-being. More promising is to move from desires to capabilities and to look at them in a long-run perspective.

To this end, the entire Chapter 2 is devoted to explaining the capability-based concept of 'human development'. Other approaches suggest making the pattern of the economic growth of advanced countries 'more human', thus forming the so-called movement going 'beyond GDP'. Our new concept builds, in particular, on the capability approach, while taking into account the economics of happiness and the need for a sustainable growth. In particular, to identify the most fundamental capabilities for development, we look at capabilities that have distinguished humans in their extraordinary evolution, thus departing from other animals. Research in different disciplines, from paleoanthropology through comparative psychology to economics, indicates a twofold typically human capability, which gives rise to the other human abilities. It is composed of *creativity*, necessary to devise new life goals, well beyond mere subsistence, and *sociality*, necessary to put in synergy the intelligence of different minds in time and space to achieve common goals. The two components need each other and together can perform the self-generating process of individual and collective development, because this is a process that makes human life meaningful and hence attractive and enjoyable. The chapter concludes by illustrating how ill-beings arise if human development weakens due to either less sociality, thus approaching the opportunistic behaviour typical of *Homo economicus*, or less creativity, thus approaching the conformist behaviour typical of *Homo sociologicus*.

Chapter 3 adopts the concept of 'human development' thus characterised to explain why economic growth, driven by market forces in the advanced countries, can deteriorate well-being in the long run. The argument follows some channels and steps, and for each of them, a variety of evidence from the recent literature is reported or cited. On the demand side, economic growth is recognised as responsible for cyclical instability and inequality (with low mobility), and both of them, in turn, increase insecurity and frustrate people's aspirations. As a result, the demand for more secure economic conditions becomes so urgent that it diverts attention from more ambitious life goals, as typical of human development. On the supply side, the parallel channel stemming from economic growth offers consumption products at ever-diminishing costs in terms of (working) time relative to human development, which must remain time-intensive (thus applying the Baumol law). People are thus increasingly induced to consume rather than invest in human development. But enjoyment from consumption is temporary and vulnerable to any external frustrating shock. Recently, the production of high-tech consumption products has even turned such tendency towards consumerism into an addiction, albeit a 'mild' one, thus making the declining trend in well-being more likely.

To further substantiate these arguments, the second part of Chapter 3 shows examples of central importance in people's lives, with a special attention to the case of the United States. It will thus become evident that worrying conditions have worsened in the job places for workers, at school for students, at home for children, and on the product market for consumers prone to addiction.

Chapter 4 takes an optimistic stance. It first identifies the lights for a long-term human recovery from the tragedy of the COVID-19 pandemic, and then it provides a framework for the action of individuals and governments to make the human development a priority over economic growth. The framework includes three types of actions: *relaxing the constrains* on human development, such as absolute and relative deprivations, lack of physical and mental health; directly *promoting* human development by focusing on school and parental education and on people's work and free time; and *defending* human development from producers' pressure, which, by means of digital platforms, have become especially intrusive in people's lives. The chapter concludes by observing how prioritising human development can improve the pattern of economic growth in terms of structure, equality, employment, and environmental sustainability.

It could be observed that a future world in which human development is the final goal and economic growth the means for it is a daydream. However, current trends can lead us to a nightmare, in which the room for human action will shrink drastically. This contrast can only be described by resorting to a bit of fiction, as only an Epilogue at the end of the book can play.

Prologue

It was 1930 when John Maynard Keynes surprised his audience by talking about what could happen after the great economic depression of those days. He ventured to predict not only an extraordinary economic growth but also what human life would be like 100 years ahead. He thus proposed a turn from the then prevailing pessimism about the pain of massive unemployment and poverty into optimism about one of the greatest opportunities in human history that their grandchildren could seize. His focus was on the United Kingdom and other advanced market economies as pioneers for the rest of the world.

Keynes made three interrelated predictions, which have been received very differently by commentators. The first prediction has been widely acknowledged, while the second has been harshly criticised. The third has been ignored, and this is curious because it gave full meaning to the first two.

The first and acclaimed prediction was that in 100 years, technical progress would have raised the standard of living so much as to solve the economic problem, namely to satisfy people's "absolute needs". This achievement would be comparable to the progress that early humans made sometimes before the last ice age because the "struggle for subsistence" has always been the "most pressing problem of the human race". The second and criticised prediction was that, thanks to such technical progress, the working time required to ensure subsistence, that is "to satisfy the old Adam in most of us", would have dramatically fallen, down to a few hours a day, thus extending free time. Frequent criticism has been that standard working hours did not drop that much, while the urge to work more seems ceaseless. The third and ignored prediction was that such extended free time would have posed a challenge: people, having secured the goods necessary to live, would have to envision and pursue some other life purposes to use the extra time available. If not overcome, the challenge would have become a problem, a well-being problem. Indeed, Keynes predicted that

DOI: 10.4324/9781003241676-2

some people would have run into "semi-pathological propensities" by maintaining money-making as their ultimate purpose, which would have been unnecessary in such a changed world. Some other people would have fallen into depression and anxiety because they would have found leisure boring and daily life severely deprived from meaning.

But Keynes was eventually optimistic for such extraordinary opportunity that humanity would have. Having gained "freedom from pressing economic care", he predicted that "we will map out for ourselves a plan of life quite otherwise than" what tradition would suggest, as people will be able to "cultivate into a fuller perfection, the art of life itself and do not sell themselves for the means of life".

The third prediction was as amazing as it now prompts questions. Was Keynes too much concerned about the well-being problem that advanced economies would encounter in the future? Is the rush to work to increase the command over material resources inherent in human nature? Is the alternative suggested by Keynes of "cultivat[ing] the art of life" naive, snobbish or vague, and thus ineffective both for interpreting facts and for prescribing how to solve the problem of well-being?

1 Economic growth and people's well-being in advanced countries

1.1 Economic growth and unsuccessful growth policies in advanced countries

Economic growth is usually expected to bring well-being to people. This is not just believed by ordinary people, but it is also predicted by economics textbooks, and it is taken for granted by politicians. The common insight is that the power to command more material resources gives people, both as individuals and organised in institutions, greater possibility of achieving their goals. Since individuals know what is best for them, or at least they can learn it over time and organise themselves accordingly, one can expect that the faster the economic growth, the more material resources and the greater people's well-being. Indeed, both casual observation and evidence in economic studies agree that richer people and richer countries are happier than their poor counterparts.

The type of economic growth most established because prolonged over time is that of advanced countries, which is characterised by the priority given to market forces within democratic rule of law. Market forces operate as a powerful engine that has been able to achieve many successes in the fight against material deprivation and disease that plagued people since historical times. However, such a pattern of economic growth also appears to have produced a number of unfortunate results over the past several decades.

First, the economic growth of these countries has decelerated to the point that some economists have even predicted the tendency to long-term stagnation. This unfortunate result follows years of policies that have attempted to revive economic growth by relying on market forces, albeit in different ways. Second, if we consider the experience of the entire set of the advanced countries, long-run economic growth is unable to predict whether and how much it tends to improve people's well-being, as subjectively reported. Third, if we consider specific experiences, more pessimistic predictions emerge, such as that of the United States (US) which, over almost half a

DOI: 10.4324/9781003241676-3

century, exhibits a decline in well-being, as variously measured. Fourth, despite the ever-diminishing scarcity of goods, social cohesion, which is a collective measure of well-being, has deteriorated, thus making the formation of governments weaker and their policies more uncertain.

These unfortunate results may appear surprising, so devoting this chapter to provide them with an empirical basis can be helpful. This section shows how economic growth has decelerated in advanced countries over the recent decades despite growth policies. The next three sections deal with the other three issues.

The deceleration of economic growth as a long-run tendency in the advanced countries can be observed in Figure 1.1. For sake of simplicity, we select the countries with both the highest gross domestic product (GDP) per capita and the highest (total) GDP in recent decades. The top six countries are thus the US, Germany, the United Kingdom (UK), France, Japan, and Italy.[1] Economic growth is defined as the trend of growth of GDP per capita, but if total factor productivity were considered, very similar results would be obtained.

Figure 1.1 illustrates that in some countries, the slowdown is minor and not always monotonic. Italy has even turned economic growth into an economic decline, as growth rates went from positive to negative around 2000.[2] This evidence is surprising because one would expect that the 'revolution' of information and communication technology (ICT), together with markets globalisation, would have spurred growth since, say, the turn of the new millennium. Only a hump appears instead in the case of the UK.

Progress in technology and science has slowed in the recent decades by many measures, such as the number of patents and major innovators, crop yields, life expectancy, pharmaceutical medicines, and the growth of chip power, known as Moore's law (Cowen & Southwood 2021). Also, the number of researchers who have been employed to produce more powerful chips, more crops per acre, and more medicines has increased exponentially (Bloom et al. 2017). In other words, more and more researchers were needed to produce fewer and fewer technological innovations. Moreover, growth of researchers ultimately depends on population growth, which is likely to decelerate in the future (Jones 2021).

The deceleration of economic growth over the long run has not gone unnoticed by governments. On the contrary, Ronald Reagan and Mrs Margaret Thatcher were elected in the 1980s as the president of the US and, respectively, the prime minister of the UK, and both of them took action in the attempt to revive economic growth. They initiated a new policy of liberalisation of the product, the labour, and especially the financial markets (Deeg 2012). They relied on private initiative to produce, to hire and fire

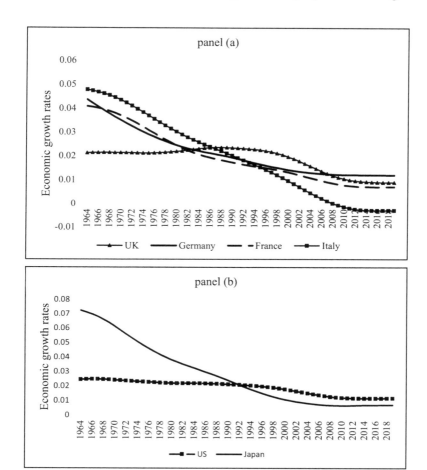

Figure 1.1 The deceleration of the economic growth in the UK, Germany, France, and Italy in panel (a) and in the US and Japan in panel (b), 1964–2019

Notes: The growth rates are obtained as the difference of the logarithms of the GDP per capita trend in 2011 US$. The trends are obtained by using the Hodrick-Prescott filter ($\lambda = 6.25$).

Source: Our elaboration from the Penn World Tables 10.0.

labour, and to lend and borrow money, i.e., they relied on market forces rather than on state regulation and intervention.

It is difficult to disentangle the effects of these policies from the effects of the ICT revolution that erupted shortly after. But overall, it can be observed that economic growth in the US slightly revives for a decade after the mid-1990s (see Figure 1.1 panel (b)). A contribution also came from China's access to the World Trade Organisation in 2001, which was favoured by the US administration and which opened a new wave of market globalisation. After a few years, however, productivity has started to decelerate again.

The policy for economic growth changed over the years, especially in the US (Covarrubias et al. 2019). Starting with the George H.W. Bush and Barack Obama administrations, particular attention has been paid to fostering ICT innovations by increasing patent protection and by weakening the enforcement of antitrust legislation to favour scale efficiency. The growth policy maintained its market orientation as prices of new products fell, and their quality improved but at the cost of the concentration of production (Grullon et al. 2019; Akcigit & Ates 2021; Aridi & Petrovcic 2019). Leaving applied technological progress in a few private hands was expected to push the frontier considerably forward, so that the value thus created would have 'trickled down' onto the rest of the economy.

However, as is evident from Figure 1.1, neither the liberalisation policies of the markets, which brought an abnormal expansion of the financial markets, nor the protection of innovations in large productive concentrations have solved the problem of the deceleration of economic growth in advanced countries. On the contrary, the rise of big corporations, in particular in the ICT sectors, has raised new problems.

At first, the fierce competition to expand the market shares of new products characterised by large efficiencies of scale and, in particular, by the use of proprietary data, pushed the technological frontier forward, but also generated the so-called 'winner-takes-all' firms. But this fact has then slowed the spread of new technologies and as a consequence has decelerated overall economic growth. In fact, the gap between the leading firms and the followers started to enlarge in the US economy as well as in other advance countries. Leading companies concentrated both total and unitary profits, thus making it possible to erect barriers by acquiring patents and competing firms to exploit initial economies rather than increasing directly productive investments. The globalisation of markets made off-shoring convenient, so that even the geographical gap between the leading firms and the rest of the economy hindered the diffusion of technology, thus failing to help the revival of economic growth (Akcigit & Ates 2021; Andrews et al. 2016; Grullon et al. 2019).

Predictions of *future* long-run economic growth, elaborated even before the COVID-19 pandemic, are rather bleak. According to some authoritative institutions and researchers, advanced countries await a new kind of economic depression. Different from the Great Depression of the 1930s, we might not expect mounting unemployment but instead a trend of very low rate of growth and persistent relative poverty. For example, Robert Gordon

(2014) predicted a rate of growth of GDP per capita of 0.9% for the United States and 0.2% for the real disposable income of the bottom 99% of the income distribution. The European Commission (2013) made the similar predictions for the European Union GDP per capita. Larry Summer, the Secretary of the Treasury during Bill Clinton's presidency, talked about 'secular stagnation', against which expansionary monetary policies will become ineffective because of sluggish reaction of investments (Summers 2014).[3] Expansionary fiscal policies cannot be easily maintained because public debt has already skyrocketed to high levels. Furthermore, the war in Ukraine has added uncertainty to the current turn towards the exit from the COVID-19 pandemic. Predictions must thus to be revised, because – according to experts – global stagflation has become more likely, and recession in Europe has become even more likely (Vaitilingam 2022).

These predictions are in contrast to the great optimism of scientists and researchers who work on the new technologies, such as the artificial intelligence, mini-robots, and new materials (see, e.g., Pratt 2015). They promise a technological advance that cannot fail to have a positive impact on growth because it will push the technological frontier forward, so that all countries will take great benefit. Unfortunately, the predicted innovations do not seem to have the same pervasive power in the economy as past innovations, such as electricity and the internal combustion engine (Gordon 2014). The optimistic prediction that new technologies have not yet unfolded the positive effects on growth and will have exceptional acceleration effects in the future (Brynjolfsson et al. 2017) has not passed some authoritative tests (Nordhaus 2015). Indeed, even the most advanced promise of technological progress, i.e.,

> the automation of the idea production, . . . has been occurring for the past hundred years or more – consider the massive improvement in the tools for conducting research, including computers, lasers, laboratories, the internet, etc. Yet growth rates in the United States have not increased.
>
> (Jones 2021:33)

1.2   Does economic growth predict people's well-being in the advanced countries?

The attempts to revive economic growth from the deceleration of recent decades relied on the confidence that higher economic growth would have brought better well-being to people. The available evidence shows, however, that such confidence is ill-founded because the relationship between economic growth and people's well-being is far from mechanical, at least in the case of the advanced countries.

Before discussing this empirical evidence, we should clarify how to identify and measure well-being as distinct from *material* well-being. The definitions and measures for well-being are many and widely debated in many disciplines. But we can greatly simplify the matter because we are interested in *long-run changes in the average well-being of large samples of people*. A suitable measure for this purpose is 'life satisfaction', which measures individuals' perceived or subjective well-being that is obtained from survey questions like "All things considered, how satisfied are you with your life as a whole these days?", with integer response options from 1 (=dissatisfied) to 10 (=satisfied). Another used measure of subjective well-being is 'happiness', which is obtained from survey questions like "Taking all things together, how would you say things are these days – would you say you are very happy, pretty happy, or not too happy?".[4] 'Life satisfaction' is a more evaluative and less emotional measure than 'happiness', and it is thus preferred if both are available.[5] Focusing on long-run changes and on averages of large samples of people greatly reduces the biases typical of the subjective measures. Nevertheless, we will also refer to other more specific measures, such as symptoms of depression, and objective measures, such as somatic markers, when this is possible (Pugno 2016:Ch.1).

The measures of subjective well-being have a number of relevant properties. They can be easily used in national surveys and are in fact available for large samples in many countries and, fortunately, for years far back in time. They are synthetic measures that avoid the problem of weighting the many aspects that may make a satisfying life. They contain valid information for comparisons over time for groups of people, as proved by more than 30 years of intense research in happiness economics. They are linked to objective measures of mental and physical health, as evidenced by scientific research in the laboratory and in the field.[6]

If we look at the studies that specifically test whether economic growth is able to predict improvements of people's subjective well-being in advanced countries, we find an overall negative conclusion. Specifically, economic growth, measured as trend of GDP per capita over spans of time of more than 12 years, is not correlated with the corresponding trend of subjective well-being in a sample of 21 advanced countries within the 1981–2013 period (Easterlin 2017).[7] This result is confirmed for longer periods, for a different statistical source, and for larger samples (Easterlin & O'Connor 2020).[8] Other more accurate tests are possible for the European countries because more information is available, and the period considered can be extended back, in some cases, to 1973. For example, the impact of economic growth on life satisfaction is not statistically significant in the case of the sample, including the Northern and Western European countries, while only the sample of the less rich countries, which include the Eastern and Southern

European countries (and Ireland), exhibits a significant impact (Kaiser & Vendrik 2019).[9]

Therefore, the available evidence shows that economic growth is not able to predict whether people's well-being is also improving or not, provided that a long period of time is considered, i.e., longer than the usual phase of cyclical recovery. This result is especially robust for the richest countries, although some evidence is also available for less advanced countries (Easterlin & O'Connor 2020).

This is surprising because casual observation and many findings confirm that richer countries (and richer people within countries) report higher subjective well-being than poorer countries (and poorer people) at a certain point in time. A contrast thus emerges between the case of a growing income over a long period of time for a country (or a group of individuals) and the case of a higher income in the comparison among countries (or individuals) at a certain date. Only in this second case is the prediction of a better subjective well-being warranted.[10] This contrast is known as the 'Easterlin paradox', so named for its discoverer in the mid-1970s (Easterlin 1974).

By looking at the long-run growth of individual countries rather than country samples, even more interesting evidence emerges. If only long periods are considered to have more reliable results, i.e., since 1973, then economic growth does not significantly predict improvements of life satisfaction in France, West Germany, Denmark, the Netherlands, Belgium, and Ireland, while it significantly predicts *declining* life satisfaction in the UK and rising life satisfaction only in Italy (Kaiser & Vendrik 2019).[11] For Japan, only fragmentary data exist, but they are sufficient to show an interesting turn: economic growth in the period 1958–1991 was associated with an improving subjective well-being, but the very low growth in the period 1992–2007 was associated with *declining* subjective well-being (Easterlin & Sawangfa 2010).

The cases of the UK and Japan suggest the hypothesis that when the economy is mature, economic growth, though low, may predict a *declining* subjective well-being.[12] This hypothesis is confirmed by two other cases: Italy and the US. The case of Italy is surprising because it has taken this pattern only in the most recent decades. It is also interesting because observing how the relationship with life satisfaction is altered provides an insight into what could happen if the major advanced countries followed the same turn in growth. The case of the US is even more interesting because it could tell us about the future of well-being in Europe and then in other countries of the world. In this case, thanks to abundance of data, the decline in well-being can be demonstrated not only with the evidence on subjective well-being but also with much other evidence.

We now give some space to the case of Italy, while the next section will show more details for the case of the US.

The Italian economic development after the Second World War displays a rather peculiar pattern. In a first period of about four decades, Italy shows exceptional growth rates, thus catching up the most advanced countries of Europe. In a second period of about a decade, it significantly reduces growth rates, thus sharing similar opulence with these countries. In a third period of nearly two decades, the Italian economy declined, thus moving away from Europe. This pattern of the Italian economic development is evident in panel (a) of Figure 1.2 (which, however, cuts the very initial years for comparison purpose with the next panel).[13]

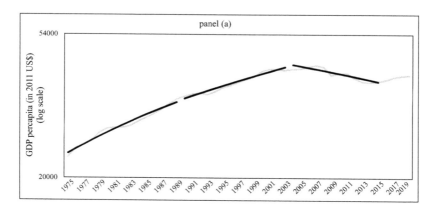

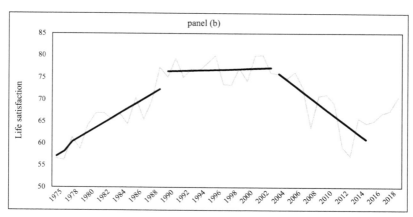

Figure 1.2 Rise and fall in: (a) real GDP per capita, and in (b) life satisfaction in Italy, 1975–2019

Notes: GDP per capita in 2011 US\$; life satisfaction = share of people 'very' and 'fairly' satisfied with life. Trends are obtained by using the Hodrick-Prescott filter ($\lambda = 6.25$).

Source: Our elaboration from the Penn World Tables 10.0 and Eurobarometer Standard Survey.

Considering these three distinct periods reveals structural breaks that are hidden by the simplistic observation that both GDP per capita and subjective well-being are higher in 2019 than in 1975. The most recent of the three periods is also a long-run period, because the economic decline extends before the cyclical world recession of 2008–2009, and it prolongs after that.

In the first period of catching-up, both GDP per capita and subjective well-being grow together, but in the middle period GDP per capita further grows, though at a lower rate, and subjective well-being ceases to improve. In the third period GDP per capita declines and subjective well-being also declines but much more. In fact, in 2014, GDP per capita was at the level of 18 years before, while subjective well-being was at the level of 27 years before!

In the years 2015–2019, there is a rebound in both economic growth and subjective well-being, but it is difficult to say that rising trends have been re-established. The pandemic crisis of 2020 and the war in Ukraine rather suggest pessimistic predictions.

In conclusion, the cases of the UK, Japan, and Italy show that the deceleration of economic growth may bring a decline in people's well-being even if the economy maintains positive growth. The case of Italy in particular shows that turning economic growth into de-growth can *especially* deteriorate well-being.

1.3   The decline of well-being in the United States

Very alarming books written by economists, psychologists, and philosophers have recently appeared on the same issue: the dramatic deterioration of the social situation in the US for several years. According to one book, inequalities are dividing the US, not just inequalities in economic conditions but also in hope, security, and aspirations, which are important for people to invest in themselves (Graham 2017). Another book documents that deaths of despair from suicide, drug overdose, and alcoholism have increased so much in the recent two decades that life expectancy was eventually reduced, much like a war would have occurred in the US (Case & Deaton 2020). A third book takes a different perspective by observing that the generation born after 1995 is no longer interested in activities that would form their adult responsibility, such as schooling, pay work, meeting friends, and even dating, while, since 2011, it exhibits a skyrocketing rise of suicides (Twenge 2017).[14]

The US is not as anomalous as it might seem. Since it is by far the leader in technology and the biggest economy of the Western world, it suggests to other countries an irresistible route for economic development, which includes opportunities but also conditions. Europe, in particular, broadly adopts US technology and grows by largely following changes of the US productive organisation. It should be recognised that many European countries, such as Germany and France but not the UK and Japan, still maintain important peculiarities that limit the free functioning of markets typical of the US by organising some 'coordination' in industrial relation, in corporate governance, and in financial system (Hall & Soskice 2001). Nevertheless, the growing free market conditions established in the US have deeply affected the entire Western world. It is sufficient to recall how the liberalisation of the financial markets that started in the US has conditioned not only business but also the economic policies of other countries (Bruno & De Bonis 2009). Or how Reagan's so-called 'supply-side economics' exported to other governments the practice of dropping taxation and privatising public enterprises. Or how the labour market in Europe approached the US standard of flexibility over the past 30 years. Therefore, the case of the US is still particularly interesting for countries on the other side of the Atlantic, and, in particular, it could help to understand their future trends.

The US is the plain paradoxical example of a growing economy with a declining trend of well-being. Only very early and unconfirmed evidence for the mid-1940s to mid-1950s period shows an increasing subjective well-being (Easterlin 1974), but after that date, all evidence shows a declining trend. This is proved for both 'life satisfaction' in the period 1985–2005 (Herbst 2011), and 'happiness' since 1976. This is proved for the data reporting the share of 'very happy' population aged 18 or over, or reporting their mean level of happiness (Stevenson & Wolfers 2008; Blanchflower & Oswald 2019; Bartolini et al. 2013).[15]

To give an idea, the decline of subjective well-being in the US population is represented in Figure 1.3 using both actual data and the estimated trend over the entire 1973–2019 period. The striking feature of the trend is that it points downward without any significant break despite short-run fluctuations.[16]

The declining trend in the well-being of the US is paradoxical because GDP per capita in real terms more than doubled over the same period. This case is more paradoxical than the original case discovered by Easterlin in which the trend of subjective well-being of the US appeared flat (Pugno 2019).

Many studies attempted to resolve the Easterlin paradox, often using the 'relative income' effect. According to such effect, well-being is deflated by comparing one's income with that of others, so that the gap can remain constant even when everyone's income increases (Clark et al. 2008). But explaining why well-being declines as income increases is a trickier matter, so that we must first be sure that well-being is actually declining, at least in the US. For this purpose, we will consider measures other than subjective well-being.

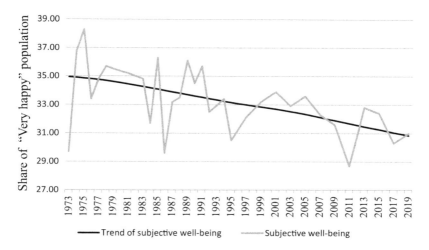

Figure 1.3 Declining subjective well-being in the US, 1973–2019

Notes: Subjective well-being = share of the 'very happy' population. The trend is obtained by using the Hodrick-Prescott filter (λ = 6.25).

Source: Our elaborations from the General Social Survey.

The extreme and reversed measure of well-being, i.e., ill-being, is the rate of suicides per 100,000 of population. In the US, this rate increased in the 1970s, until it began to decrease in the mid-1980s for the older age group and a few years later for the younger age group, and then it began to gradually increase again, with an acceleration starting in 2006 until it reached with the preceding peak in 2018.[17] The introduction of antidepressants seems to be a factor explaining the decrease in the middle of the period considered, so the recent acceleration is especially worrying, as the use of antidepressants has been increased by a multiple (Pratt et al. 2011). The peculiarity of the recent acceleration is that it is driven by suicides among 15- to 24-year olds, and that, for the first time, females follow the increasing trend of males.

Suicides seem to affect a tiny minority, but suicide attempts are 10 times that, and suicide ideations are an even higher multiple. Moreover, suicides are largely underreported. Estimates that also include 'non-suicide' fatalities from drug self-intoxication, for example, show that the rate is more than double in 2018 than the rate of reported suicides, after having increased three times faster since 1999.

Measures on mental health confirm and extend the evidence on suicides. A psychology article collected 141 samples of US college students ranging from 1938 to 2007 from the specialised literature and examined the time changes in the frequency of eight clinical psychopathologies. It thus showed that all psychopathologies have progressively become more frequent, including major depression (Twenge et al. 2010).[18] By adopting a different method of detection of major depression in the population on the basis of nationally representative samples, two articles showed that the frequency of this mental disorder has increased from 1991 to 2002, has remained stable until 2010, and then has started to increase again until 2018, especially among young people aged 12–25 (Compton et al. 2006; Weinberger et al. 2018).[19]

Milder mental problems are more difficult to accurately detect over time. Nevertheless, anxiety very likely became more common in the US during the 1952–2017 period (Twenge 2000; Booth et al. 2016; Duffy et al. 2019).[20] A similar greater prevalence seem concerning other somatic and behavioural symptoms in adults, such as 'having trouble getting to sleep', "feeling under great pressure most of the time" (in the 1985–2005 period), and "having subjective feeling of stress, depression and emotions" (in the 1993–2019 period) (Herbst 2011; Blanchflower & Oswald 2020). Young people aged 13–18 reported mixed answers to national surveys before the early 2010s because they exhibited a rising life satisfaction but worse somatic symptoms, such as "having difficulty of thinking, concentrating, remembering, and learning" (Twenge 2016; Twenge et al. 2016). Over the past decade, however, life satisfaction and happiness reported by this young population group have declined, thus aligning the trend with that of the other age groups (Twenge et al. 2018; Keyes et al. 2019).

Therefore, the decline of the average well-being of the population in the US over a period of more than 40 years is more a fact than a conjecture. The rate of decline may have improved for some time and for some population groups, but the overall deterioration is confirmed by a number of measures. Taking the past 20 years, the evidence of a severe deterioration is as strong as it is summarised by the disappointing evidence of people's overall health, which eventually turn into a rise in mortality and even a reduction of life expectancy (Greaney et al. 2019; Ruhm 2020; Wolf & Schoomaker 2019), thus making the first economy in the world the last country for the health of its citizens, including children, in the ranking of the Western world (Blanchflower & Oswald 2019; UNICEF 2017).[21]

1.4   Economic growth and the deterioration of social cohesion

The Great Recession of 2008–2009 contributed to the deceleration of the long-run economic growth in the advanced countries due to its severity and, especially in some cases, to its time length. Unemployment increased, albeit far less than in the Great Depression of the 1930s, but the bad news was the rise of precarious and low-paid jobs. The crisis thus aggravated workers' conditions, as competition of Chinese products already hit some sectors and immigrants already pressed on the labour market.

Therefore, the crisis affected workers very differently, depending on their education, production sectors, and location. Governments took remedial measures, as already mentioned, but failed to reassure the population's expectation for their future. It is thus not surprising that dissatisfaction and distrust in governments and traditional political parties mounted in some sections of the population, so that these demanded for policies aimed at their immediate and particular needs. In other words, the mass demand for populism and nationalism arose in the US and Europe. The divides in the population translated into political divides, so that the loss of social cohesion has become a structural aspect, which could have long run effects.

Some studies even argue that the most dissatisfied people substituted the priority of improving their economic conditions with the priority of defending themselves against what they considered more general threats, namely governments and supporting intellectuals (often called 'the elite'), foreign countries, and immigrants. Social media, which already became popular, not only gave an effective voice to dissatisfactions but also fostered the belief that *people*, rather than 'the elite', are the true sovereign of the *nation* and that they should come first with respect to foreign populations. In this way, a new social identity has emerged as based on traditional values and contrary to social innovations, thus often replacing the identity of belonging to the working class. People's differences have become a polarisation of values, preferences, and beliefs. The emerging protest against the previous policies of markets liberalisation and in defence of traditional national identity has translated into a demand for populist and nationalist policies (Margalit 2019; Watson et al. 2022).[22]

Parties with some clear populist and nationalist characteristics have been almost synchronously successful in several advanced countries. In 2010, 2013, and 2014, the Freedom Party in the Netherlands, the Five Star Movement in Italy, and the Marine Le Pen's National Front in France gathered a multiple of their previous votes in their respective national elections. The Party for Freedom joined a governmental coalition in 2010, and the Five Star Movement together with the Lega formed the government in 2018. In Germany, the far-right party of Alternative fuer Deutschland entered for the first time the Parliament in 2017 by doubling the threshold.

But the most surprising cases of success for populists and nationalists were the US presidential election of November 2016 and the Brexit vote in June 2016. The former brought people to polarise and turned policies from liberal to protective in the international markets and against immigration.

The latter has brought the UK out of the free movement of goods and people prevailing within the European Union (EU).

Evidence on these two major cases is rather abundant. According to some evidence, in US presidential elections, counties with greater trade exposure shifted towards the Republican candidate, and in the 2016 election in particular, people with less trust in others and less engaged in social organisations more likely voted for Donald Trump. Chinese import shocks drove negative attitudes towards immigrants and minorities, while Republican candidates moved from supporting free trade in 2008 presidential election to protectionism in the following presidential election and assumed harsher stances on immigration, thus attracting more votes (Autor et al. 2020; Giuliano 2020). According to other evidence, "voting behaviour in 2016 was driven by a desire for in-group affiliation as a way of buffering against economic and cultural anxiety" (Fabian et al. 2020).

Group polarisation has thus accelerated in recent years, following a rising long-run trend. This emerges clearly, for example, by measuring polarisation as the difference between people's affect for the Republican and Democratic parties from 1980 to 2016, with the rise of the animus against the opposing party as the main force.[23] The surprising election of Trump undoubtedly benefited from the "echo chambers" effect of social media, which created networks for individuals sharing the similar political beliefs (Gorodnichenko et al. 2018).

In the case of the UK, evidence shows that individuals living in regions exposed to higher imports from low-wage countries were more critical of EU membership and international cooperation and exhibited more nationalistic sentiments, thus tending to support radical right-wing parties (Steiner & Harms 2020). Other studies confirm that individuals and areas with lower education, income, and employment or with lower life satisfaction were more likely to vote for Brexit (Becker et al. 2017). The success of the pro-leavers seems to be due to the marginal contribution of social media, which strengthened and spread their beliefs (Gorodnichenko et al. 2018).

The deterioration of social cohesion within the countries but also with other populations is also evident from the recent upsurge of hate and violence. A reliable measure of hate is the number of hate crimes defined as reported criminal offenses against a person or property motivated by an offender's bias against a race, religion, disability, sexual orientation, ethnicity, or gender. It is thus possible to analyse the quarterly changes of hate crimes from 1992 to 2017 at the county level in the US (having controlled for the trend, the terrorist attacks, and other socio-economic variables). The rapid increase coinciding with Trump's election and continuing through 2017 stands out as exceptional, when compared with the terrorist attacks of 2009 and 2015[24] and clearly driven by counties where Trump's support was greater. This evidence suggests that Trump's election validated both his divisive campaign rhetoric and the biased beliefs of a part of the Americans, who realised they were a substantial part (Edwards & Rushin 2021; Mueller & Schwarz 2018).

Hate crimes also increased rapidly, on a daily basis, in the UK, coinciding with the result of the Brexit referendum. The increase was greater and more prolonged than those following the terrorist attacks in Manchester and Finsbury Park in 2017, while also excluding the hate crimes driven by possible responses against British whites. Moreover, the increase in hate crimes in 2016 does not appear to be due to the increase in coverage of hate crimes in national newspapers (Devine 2018; see also Piatkowska & Stults 2021). Again, the evidence on the Brexit case suggests that the result of the referendum validated the biased beliefs of large sections of the population.

It is too early to evaluate the long-run costs due to socio-political polarisation and the consequent governance and policies, but some attempts already indicate worrying results. In the US, capital returns dropped in 2018 and 2019 following trade war announcements with China, so that a 1.9% reduction in investment growth over two years has been estimated (Amiti et al. 2020). Exports from the UK to the EU are expected to decline between 7.2 and 45.7 six years after Brexit has taken place, thus inducing a decline in UK's GDP of between 0.3% and 5.7% (Oberhofer & Pfaffermayr 2020).[25]

Notes

1 Canada is seventh and Australia is eighth in the ranking, and they exhibit a similar slowdown.
2 The slowdown of the economic growth is not due to mismeasurements and statistical biases (Ahmad et al. 2017 and citations therein).
3 See Fernald & Jones (2014), Piketty (2014), and Alfredsson & Malmaeus (2017) about other similar predictions on economic growth, and Teulings & Baldwin (2014) about the debate on the possible future 'secular stagnation'.
4 See, for example, the World Values Survey, the Eurobarometer Standard survey, and the General Social Survey.
5 The third measure of subjective well-being adopts the Cantril Self-Anchoring Striving Scale, according to which people rate their lives on a ladder with rungs numbered from 0 to 10, where 0, at the bottom of the ladder, equals, in their view, the worst possible life, and 10, the top rung, equals the best. This measure is used by the Gallup World Poll.
6 See, e.g., Frey & Stutzer (2002) and the *World Happiness Report* issued almost every year since 2012.
7 The dataset used is drawn from the World Values Survey, and the 21 countries are Australia, Austria, Belgium, Canada, Denmark, Finland, France, Germany, Ireland, Italy, Japan, Netherlands, New Zealand, Norway, Portugal, Spain, Sweden, Switzerland, Taiwan, the UK, and the US.

8   The period is extended to 2019, the new statistical source is the Gallup World Poll, and the extra-countries considered are Israel, Hong Kong, Greece, and Singapore.

9   These results are obtained by taking into account extra-economic common drivers of improvement in life satisfaction. The Northern and Western European countries considered are Denmark, Finland, Sweden, and Austria, Belgium, France, West Germany, Netherlands, the UK. The Eastern and Southern European countries are Bulgaria, Czech Republic, Croatia, East Germany, Estonia, Hungary, Latvia, Lithuania, Poland, Romania, Slovakia, Slovenia, Turkey, Greece, Italy, Portugal, and Spain. See also Beja (2014).

10 Recently, even this second case has been questioned. Precisely, higher GDP per capita across countries and across European regions seems to predict greater individuals' life satisfaction but only until a threshold. If GDP per capita is higher than the threshold, life satisfaction is lower (Proto & Rustichini 2013).

11 These results are obtained by controlling for the cycle, lagged life satisfaction, and other interaction terms.

12 The cross-country at-a-point-in-time perspective would suggest that a country becomes mature when it crosses the threshold of about 30,000 USD$ (2005 in purchasing power parity) (Proto & Rustichini 2013).

13 For more formal evidence, see Pugno & Sarracino (2021) and Pugno (2021).

14 See also the alarming book of the philosopher Sandel (2020).

15 The decline is also proved when happiness of the population is measured as their median level (Chen et al. 2019) to avoid the criticism leveled by Bond & Lang (2014) on ordinal measures, which, however, emerges as empirically implausible (Kaiser & Vendrik 2020).

16 The decline is statistically significant, since the 95% confidence interval is [− 0.127, − 0.0537], and the coefficient reports p=0.000. No significant single breaks emerge (Wald test=2.53, p=0.948 at 1981, which is the endogenously determined best break).

17 The national crude suicide rate rose to 14.8 in 2018, which is 1.4 times higher than the 1999 rate. The annual suicide rate increased by 1.0% between 1999 and 2006 and more than doubled to 2.3% between 2006 and 2018. All the cited evidence on suicides is drawn from McKeown et al. (2006), Ruch et al. (2019), Hedegaard et al. (2021), Rockett et al. (2021), Xiao et al. (2021).

18 This meta-analysis selects the studies that use the Minnesota Multiphasic Personality Inventory scale to detect the psychopathologies and controls for a variety of biases, thus resulting more complete than the previous more ambiguous studies.

19 Both articles adopt the *Diagnostic and Statistical Manual of Mental Disorders –* fourth edition.

20 Anxiety of university students increased in the Western countries in period 1985–2017, according to Kosic et al. (2020).

21 The UK seems to follow the US example because economic growth has been definitely positive in the most recent decades, but a variety of measures indicate a rising trend of mental problems in the population: teenage children of all social classes experienced emotional and conduct problems almost twice as frequently in 1999 than in 1974 (Collishaw et al. 2004); a similar trend emerged for depression and anxiety among British youths in the period 1986–2006 (Collishaw et al. 2010). Common mental disorders rise in the period 1993–2014, and suicidal thoughts and self-harm after 2000 (McManus et al. 2016). The rise of such psychological distress for young women in the period 1991–2008 is confirmed by

research using the General Health Questionnaire (Ross et al. 2017). Moreover, job satisfaction declined in the period 1994–2012 (Green & Tsitsianis 2005; Green et al. 2013), and happiness in children declined in the period 2009–2017 (UK Department of Education 2019) .

22 The question of whether economic or cultural factors are the most important in explaining the rise of populism is difficult to resolve because both are partially endogenous in the long run.

23 See Iyengar et al. (2019), who shows that Americans have become increasingly averse to the prospect of their children marrying those from the opposing party.

24 The attack in 2009 was at Virginia Tech, and the terrorist killed 32 people. The attack in 2015 was in Orlando, Florida, and the terrorist killed 49 people.

25 Other estimates talk about the range of 4–6% reduction of UK's GDP (Vaitilingam 2021).

References

Ahmad N, Ribarsky J, Reinsdorf M (2017) Can potential mismeasurement of the digital economy explain the post-crisis slowdown in GDP and productivity growth? *OECD Statistics Working Papers* 2017/09, OECD Publishing, Paris

Akcigit U, Ates ST (2021) Ten facts on declining business dynamism and lessons from endogenous growth theory. *American Economic Journal: Macroeconomics* 13(1):257–298

Alfredsson EC, Malmaeus JM (2017) Prospects for economic growth in the 21st century. *Economic Issues* 22:65–87

Amiti M, Kong SH, Weinstein D (2020) The effect of the U.S.-China trade war on U.S. investment. *NBER Working Paper* No. 27114. Cambridge, MA, https://www.nber.org/papers/w27114

Andrews D, Criscuolo C, Gal P (2016) The best versus the rest. *OECD Productivity Working Papers*, No. 5. OECD Publishing, Paris

Aridi A, Petrovcic U (2019) *Big Tech, Small Tech, and the Data Economy*. World Bank Group, https://openknowledge.worldbank.org/handle/10986/33124

Autor D, Dorn D, Hanson G, Majlesi K (2020) Importing political polarization? *NBER Working Paper* No. 22637. Cambridge, MA, https://www.nber.org/papers/w22637

Bartolini S, Bilancini E, Pugno M (2013) Did the decline in social connections depress Americans' happiness. *Social Indicators Research* 110(3):1033–1059

Becker SO, Thiemo F, Dennis N (2017) Who voted for Brexit? *CESifo Working Paper* No. 6438, https://www.cesifo.org/DocDL/cesifo1_wp6438.pdf

Beja EL (2014) Income growth and happiness. *International Review of Economics* 61(4):329–346

Blanchflower DG, Oswald AJ (2019) Unhappiness and pain in modern America. *Journal of Economic Literature* 57(2):358–402

Blanchflower DG, Oswald AJ (2020) Trends in extreme distress in the USA, 1993–2019. *American Journal of Public Health* 110(10):1538–1544

Bloom N, Jones CI, Van Reenen J, Webb M (2017) Are ideas getting harder to find? *NBER Working Papers* No. 23782. Cambridge, MA, https://www.nber.org/papers/w23782

Bond TN, Lang K (2014) The sad truth about happiness scales. *NBER Working Paper* No. 19950. Cambridge, MA, https://www.nber.org/papers/w19950

Booth RW, Sharma D, Leader TI (2016) The age of anxiety? It depends where you look. *Social Psychiatry and Psychiatric Epidemiology* 51:193–202

Brynjolfsson E, Rock D, Syverson C (2017) Artificial intelligence and the modern productivity paradox. *NBER Working Paper* No. 24001. Cambridge, MA, https://www.nber.org/papers/w24001

Bruno B, De Bonis R (2009) Do financial systems converge? New evidence from household financial assets in selected OECD countries. *OECD Statistics Working Papers*, No. 2009/01. Éditions OCDE, Paris

Case A, Deaton A (2020) *Deaths of Despair and the Future of Capitalism*. Princeton: Princeton University Press

Chen L-Y, Oparina E, Powdthavee N, Srisuma S (2019) Have econometric analyses of happiness data been futile? *IZA DP* No. 12152, https://docs.iza.org/dp12152.pdf

Clark AE, Frijters P, Shields M (2008) Relative income, happiness and utility. *Journal of Economic Literature* 46(1):95–144

Collishaw S, Maughan B, Goodman R (2004) Time trend in adolescent mental health. *Journal of Child Psychology and Psychiatry* 45(8):1350–1362

Collishaw S, Maughan B, Natarajan L, Pickles A (2010) Trends in adolescent emotional problems in England. *Journal of Child Psychology and Psychiatry* 51(8):885–894

Compton WM, Conway KP, Stinson SF, Grant BF (2006) Changes in the prevalence of major depression and comorbid substance use disorders in the United States between 1991–1992 and 2001–2002. *American Journal of Psychiatry* 163:2141–2147

Covarrubias M, Gutiérrez G, Philippon T (2019) From good to bad concentration? *NBER Working Paper* No. 25983. Cambridge, MA, https://www.nber.org/papers/w25983

Cowen T, Southwood B (2021) Is the rate of scientific progress slowing down? George Mason University Department of Economics. *Working Paper* No. 21–13, https://ssrn.com/abstract=3822691

Deeg R (2012) The limits of Liberalization? American capitalism at the crossroads. *Journal of European Public Policy* 19(8):1249–1268

Devine D (2018) *The UK Referendum on Membership of the European Union as a Trigger Event for Hate Crimes*. Retrieved [28 Feb. 2022] from: https://papers.ssrn.com/sol3/papers.cfm?abstract_id=3118190

Duffy ME, Twenge JM, Joiner TE (2019) Trends in mood and anxiety symptoms and suicide-related outcomes among US undergraduates, 2007–2018. *Journal of Adolescent Health* 65:590–598

Easterlin RA (1974) Does economic growth improve the human lot? In P David, M Reder (eds) *Nations and Households in Economic Growth*. New York: Academic Press, pp. 89–125

Easterlin RA (2017) Paradox lost? *Review of Behavioral Economics* 4(4):311–339

Easterlin RA, O'Connor K (2020) The Easterlin Paradox. *IZA DP* No. 13923, https://docs.iza.org/dp13923.pdf

Easterlin RA, Sawangfa O (2010). Happiness and economic growth. In E Diener, JF Helliwell, D Kahneman (eds) *International Differences in Well-Being*. Oxford: Oxford University Press, pp. 166–216

Edwards GS, Rushin S (2021) *The Effect of President Trump's Election on Hate Crimes* (January 14, 2018). Retrieved [28 Feb. 2022] from: https://ssrn.com/abstract=3102652

European Commission (2013) *Quarterly Report on the Euro Area*. Vol 12. N. 4. Luxembourg: Publications Office of the European Union

Fabian M, Agarwala M, Alexandrova A, Coyle D, Felici M (2020) Wellbeing Public Policy Needs More Theory. *Bennett Institute for Public Policy*. University of Cambridge. Retrieved [28 Feb. 2022] from: www.bennettinstitute.cam.ac.uk/media/uploads/files/WPP_needs_more_theory_working_paper.pdf

Fernald J, Jones CI (2014) The future of US economic growth. *American Economic Review: Papers & Proceedings* 104(5):44–49

Frey BS, Stutzer A (2002) What can economists learn from happiness research? *Journal of Economic Literature* 40(2):402–435

Giuliano P, Wacziarg R (2020) Who voted for Trump? *NBER Working Paper* No. 27651. Cambridge, MA, https://www.nber.org/papers/w27651

Gordon RJ (2014) The demise of U.S. economic growth. *NBER Working Paper* No. 19895. Cambridge, MA, https://www.nber.org/papers/w19895

Gorodnichenko Y, Pham T, Talavera O (2018) Social media, sentiment and public opinions. *NBER Working Paper* No. 24631. Cambridge, MA, https://www.nber.org/papers/w24631

Graham C (2017) *Happiness for All?: Unequal Hopes and Lives in Pursuit of the American Dream*. Princeton: Princeton University Press

Greaney ML, Cohen S, Blissmet BJ (2019) Age-specific trends in health-related quality of life among US adults. *Quality of Life Research* 28:3249–3257

Green F, Mostafa T, Parent-Thirion A, Vermeylen G, Van Houten G, Biletta I, Lyly-Yrjanainen M (2013) Is job quality becoming more unequal? *Industrial and Labor Relations Review* 66(4):753–784

Green F, Tsitsianis N (2005) An investigation of national trends in job satisfaction in Britain and Germany. *British Journal of Industrial Relations* 1080:401–429

Grullon G, Larken Y, Michaely R (2019) Are US industries becoming more concentrated? *Review of Finance* 23(4):697–743

Hall PA, Soskice D (2001) *Varieties of Capitalism*. Oxford: Oxford University Press

Hedegaard H, Curtin SC, Warner M (2021) Suicide mortality in the United States, 1999–2019. *NCHS Data Brief, No. 398*, February, https://www.cdc.gov/nchs/data/databriefs/db398-H.pdfhttps://www.cdc.gov/nchs/data/databriefs/db398-H.pdf

Herbst CM (2011) Paradoxical decline? *Journal of Economic Psychology* 32:773–788

Iyengar S, Lelkes Y, Levendusky M, Malhotra N, Westwood SJ (2019) The origins and consequences of affective polarization in the United States. *Annual Review of Political Science* 22:129–146

Jones CJ (2021) The past and future of economic growth. *NBER Working Paper* No. 29126. Cambridge, MA, https://www.nber.org/papers/w29126

Kaiser CF, Vendrik MCM (2019) Different versions of the Easterlin Paradox. In M Rojas (ed) *The Economics of Happiness*. Springer, Cham, Switzerland, pp. 27–55

Kaiser CF, Vendrik MCM (2020) How threatening are transformations of happiness scales to subjective wellbeing research? *IZA DP* No. 13905, https://docs.iza.org/dp13905.pdf

Keyes M, Gary D, O'Malley PM, Hamilton A, Schulenberg J (2019) Recent increases in depressive symptoms among US adolescents. *Social Psychiatry and Psychiatric Epidemiology* 54(8):987–996

Kosic A, Lindholm P, Järvholm K, Hedman-Lagerlöf E, Axelsson E (2020) Three decades of increase in health anxiety. *Journal of Anxiety Disorders* 71:102208

Margalit Y (2019) Economic insecurity and the causes of populism, reconsidered. *Journal of Economic Perspectives* 33(4):152–170

McKeown RE, Cuffe SP, Schulz RM (2006) US suicide rates by age group, 1970–2002. *American Journal of Public Health* 96:10

McManus S, Bebbington PE, Jenkins R, Brugha T (2016) *Mental Health and Wellbeing in England*. Leed, UK: NHS Digital

Mueller K, Schwarz C (2018) *From Hashtag to Hate Crime* (July 24, 2020). Retrieved [28 Feb. 2022] from: https://ssrn.com/abstract=3149103

Nordhaus WD (2015) Are we approaching an economic singularity? *NBER Working Paper* No. 21547. Cambridge, MA, https://www.nber.org/papers/w21547

Oberhofer H, Pfaffermayr M (2020) Estimating the trade and welfare effects of Brexit. *Canadian Journal of Economics* 54(1):338–375

Piatkowska SJ, Stults BS (2021) Brexit, terrorist attacks, and hate crime. *Social Problems* (forthcoming)

Piketty T (2014) *Capital*. Cambridge, MA: Harvard University Press

Pratt GA (2015) Is a Cambrian explosion coming for robotics? *Journal of Economic Perspectives* 29:51–60

Pratt LA, Brody DJ, Gu Q (2011) Antidepressant use in persons aged 12 and over. *NCHS Data Brief* No. 76, October, https://pubmed.ncbi.nlm.nih.gov/22617183/

Proto E, Rustichini A (2013) A reassessment of the relationship between GDP and life satisfaction. *PLoS ONE* 8(11):e79358

Pugno M (2016) *On the Foundations of Happiness in Economics*. London: Routledge

Pugno M (2019) Why the Easterlin paradox? The Scitovsky hypothesis. In M Rojas (ed) *The Economics of Happiness*. Cham (Switzerland): Springer, Ch. 7, pp. 157–170

Pugno, M (2021) Italy's parabolas of GDP and subjective well-being: the role of education. *MPRA paper*, n. 107948, https://mpra.ub.uni-muenchen.de/107948/1/MPRA_paper_107948.pdf

Pugno M, Sarracino F (2021) Structural changes in economic growth and wellbeing. The case of Italy's parabola. *Social Indicators Research* 158:801–838

Rockett IRH, Caine ED, Banerjee A (2021) Fatal self-injury in the United States. *EClinicalMedicine* 32:100741

Ross A, Kelly Y, Sacker A (2017) Time trends in mental well-being. *Social Psychiatry and Psychiatric Epidemiology* 52:1147–1158

Ruch DA, Sheftall AH, Schlagbaum P, Rausch J, Campo JV, Bridge JA (2019) Trends in suicide among youth aged 10 to 19 years in the United States. *JAMA Netw Open* 2(5):e193886

Ruhm CJ (2020) Living and dying in America. *NBER Working Papers* No. 28358. Cambridge, MA, https://www.nber.org/papers/w28358

Sandel MJ (2020) *The Tyranny of Merit*. London: Penguin

Steiner ND, Harms P (2020). Local trade shocks and the nationalist backlash in political attitudes. Gutenberg School of Management and Economics, *Discussion Paper* No. 2014, https://download.uni-mainz.de/RePEc/pdf/Discussion_Paper_2014.pdf

Stevenson B, Wolfers J (2008) Economic growth and happiness. *Brookings Papers on Economic Activity* May:1–87

Summers, L (2014), "US Economic Prospects: Secular Stagnation, Hysteresis and the Zero Lower Bound", speech delivered to the National Association for Business Economics' *Economic Policy Conference*, 24 February, Arlington, USA

Teulings C, Baldwin R (2014). *Secular Stagnation*. London: CEPR

Twenge JM (2000) The age of anxiety? *Journal of Personality and Social Psychology* 79(6):1007–1021

Twenge JM (2016) Time period and birth cohort differences in depressive symptoms in the U.S., 1982–2013. *Social Indicators Research* 121:437–454

Twenge JM (2017) *iGen: Why Today's Super-connected Kids Are Growing up Less Rebellious, More Tolerant, Less Happy – And Completely Unprepared for Adulthood*. New York: Atria Books

Twenge JM, Gentile B, DeWall CN, Ma DS, Lacefield K, Schurtz DR (2010) Birth cohort increases in psychopathology among young Americans, 1938–2007. *Clinical Psychology Review* 30:145–154

Twenge JM, Martin GN, Campbell WK (2018) Decreases in psychological well-being among American adolescents after 2012 and links to screen time during the rise of smartphone technology. *Emotion* 18:765–780

Twenge JM, Sherman RA, Lyubomirsky S (2016) More happiness for young people and less for mature adults. *Social Psychological and Personality Science* 7:131–141

UK Department of Education (2019) *State of the Nation 2019: Children and Young People's Wellbeing*. Retrieved [28 Feb. 2022] from: www.gov.uk/government/publications

UNICEF (2017) *Children in a Digital World*. New York: UNICEF

Vaitilingam R (2021) After Brexit: The impacts on the UK and EU economies by 2030. *LSE Business Review*. Retrieved [28 Feb. 2022] from: http://eprints.lse.ac.uk/108693/

Vaitilingam R (2022) Economic consequences of Russia's invasion of Ukraine. *VoxEu CEPR*. Retrieved [25 Mar. 2022] from: https://voxeu.org/article/economic-consequences-war-ukraine-igm-forum-survey

Watson B, Law S, Osberg L (2022) Are populists insecure about themselves or about their country? *Social Indicators Research* 159(2):667–705

Weinberger AH, Gbedemah M, Martinez AM, Nash D (2018) Trends in depression prevalence in the USA from 2005 to 2015. *Psychological Medicine* 48(8):1308–1315

Woolf SH, Schoomaker H (2019) Life expectancy and mortality in the US, 1959–2017. *JAMA* 322(20):1996–2016

Xiao Y, Cerel J, Mann JJ (2021) Temporal trends in suicidal ideation and attempts among US adolescents by sex and race/ethnicity. *Jama Network Open* 4(6):e2113513

2 Human development and well-being

2.1 In search of a human development that ensures well-being

Prioritising economic growth could be justified by arguing that it offers ever-expanding opportunities for satisfying people's desires. Economics textbooks explain that the market is very efficient in exploiting available technology to provide the best options to consumers, who can thus pursue well-being by exercising their freedom of choice. However, as shown in Chapter 1, the world's largest affluent country with a highly developed market economy and liberal institutions, namely the United States, exhibits *declining* well-being over many decades, while gross domestic product (GDP) has grown by a multiple. Moreover, social divisions within the country are worsening dangerously, as evident from the recent protests against the anti–COVID-19 pandemic measures and from the attacks on democratic institutions in the election of the president.

Indeed, a movement to go 'beyond GDP' has been growing for several years now, having recognised that economic growth is insufficient to ensure social progress and individual well-being, and it becomes even harmful when it degrades the environment. The research for more accurate indicators of human progress has thus skyrocketed, and clear recommendations have emerged. For example, the United Nations Development Program (UNDP) recommends pursuing education and health as specific goals in addition to economic growth; the so-called 'economics of happiness' in its most hedonistic version recommends pursuing what closely correlates with people's subjective well-being; environmentalists recommend that the pattern of economic growth should change to no longer degrade the environment.

However, an effective remedial recommendation needs a preliminary explanation of the failures of economic growth in affluent countries. The interpretation of past events should precede and complement the prescriptions. Thereby, a number of questions arises and should first be addressed: if

DOI: 10.4324/9781003241676-4

people were so free to choose what is best for them, why has not economic growth increased well-being? If people had chosen in a wrong way, why didn't they correct their errors in the long run? If governments and other institutions have been trapped in inefficient decisions, why don't people press for a change? Being able to learn more and more easily from the history of the development of civilisations and having more and more opportunities for knowledge, movement, and contacts with others, why do most people refrain from broadening their interests, challenging their abilities, and aspiring to new and ambitious goals, even when they have no subsistence problems?

The present book intends to take some steps forward to answer these questions. To such end, it proposes to go beyond approaches that go 'beyond GDP'. In fact, we will observe that it is not enough to consider GDP (as well as its growth) necessary but not sufficient to ensure people's well-being and simply add other relevant variables or constraints. Our central arguments will be that economic growth in advanced market economies can be itself responsible for the tendential reduction in the well-being of the population and their cohesion, and that the reason for these outcomes lies in the deterioration of *human development*. Therefore, to ensure increases in people's well-being, it will be necessary to prioritise human development over economic growth. The effect will be to shape economic growth rather than turning it into degrowth.

The remainder of this section is devoted to the insights and weaknesses of approaches that go 'beyond GDP', while subsequent sections will present and discuss the new concept of 'human development' that plays a key role in the book.

The main approaches that intend to go 'beyond GDP' are three: the approach of *Human Development Reports* by the UNDP, the approach of people's life satisfaction as the final policy goal, and the environmentalist approach.

In its reports, the UNDP argues that "human development [defined as] a process of enlarging people's choices" should be taken as the ultimate end. It further specifies that "the three essential choices for people are to lead a long and healthy life, to acquire knowledge and to have access to the resources needed for a decent standard of living", while other freedoms and capabilities are also "highly valued by many people" (UNDP 1997:13–14).[1] Economic growth is thus considered a necessary but not sufficient means for human development because supplementary actions must guarantee people a "long and healthy life", education, and "a decent standard of living".

This is a significant step forward, especially because the importance of people's capabilities is recognised. However, there are two weaknesses in this approach. First, the aforementioned choices of people appear rather like their general aspirations. Indeed, when people actually choose in their daily life, they also reflect preferences other than those for health and learning, even if their living standard is more than decent (Pugno 2008a).[2] Cases of addiction, including behavioural addiction, and myopia in early school leaving can be mentioned (see section 3.5). Second, the approach overlooks the fact that the governments should choose to augment intervention in the markets to realise the three people's general aspirations. In fact, producers in market economies have not the goal of maximising education or health of the entire population, as the experience of the COVID-19 pandemic has shown. Producers' goal is to maximise profits and sales, and to such goal, they aim to change people's preferences even if these diverge from people's general aspirations.

Another approach that intends to go beyond GDP is the approach of life satisfaction (or happiness) as the final goal for both policy-makers and individuals (see, e.g., Frijters et al. 2020). This is a strictly empirical approach as it first ascertains the validity and reliability of life satisfaction as a measure of people's well-being, and then it studies which variables best correlate with life satisfaction by applying multivariate econometric analysis. Various techniques are increasingly adopted to interpret correlation as causation (instrumental variable estimation, difference-in-difference technique, etc.). The samples used in the estimations are usually large, and the variables used are often proxies of the phenomenon to be captured. The evidence thus obtained can provide a standard for evaluating policies and individual actions in their effectiveness of improving well-being.

The mass of evidence produced by this approach has proved that life satisfaction is not as elusive a measure as it appears and that some correlates, such as being employed, in good health, married, richer than others, and not middle-aged, are significant and robust in cross-section and panel analyses. This approach has enormously advanced our knowledge about people's well-being and correlates, and in particular, it has demonstrated how small the impact of income is, albeit statistically very significant.

However, not even this approach is without weaknesses. First of all, the tests are applied to equations in too reduced form, often a single equation, with the consequence that the resulting evidence can be consistent with various theoretical explanations, and it can even be misleading. For example, education frequently appears as an unimportant or insignificant partial correlate with life satisfaction. But a study using a structural equation model shows that the positive effect of education on life satisfaction is mostly indirect, through income, employment, marriage, and health (Powdthavee et al. 2015).

The large size of the samples used is often a necessity to capture the significance of the correlates. Nevertheless, the total variance explained by the correlates is generally quite low, thus revealing again that there is room to explain life satisfaction more accurately. Proceeding with this evidence-driven econometric approach to test possible causation chains can still lead to interesting results. But every result inconsistent with the previous ones requires multiplying the econometric estimates and needing for other underlying surveys, and this makes the approach rather unwieldy.

Another weakness concerns the approximation with which the measure of life satisfaction and the other measures of subjective well-being, such as happiness and the Cantril ladder of life, capture the phenomenon of people's well-being.[3] People's answer to the question about their life satisfaction is not necessarily the best predictor of their well-being. The most studied alternative measures that have proven better in several cases relate to measures of how people feel functioning. As it will be seen later, these measures, often called eudaimonic, report people's answers about meaning and purpose in their life, interest in new things, and feeling competent and capable of having good relationships. Indeed, various evidence in psychology and economics shows that one or more eudaimonic measures are better predictors of people's health markers, diseases, and even mortality than subjective well-being measures (Ryff et al. 2004; Boyle et al. 2009; Bachelet et al. 2020).

The environmental approach is based on a problem that economic growth cannot avoid: the growing probability that environmental disasters will seriously affect people's well-being as production and consumption increase. Pro-environmental policies have already been implemented, but disasters are already multiplying. The need to raise the priority of environmental protection over economic growth is not easily contested, as it is possible to modify production and consumption for this purpose.

However, since the environment has characteristics of public good, and actions to protect it are costly, individuals and governments would like to pass such protection onto others, that is, to free ride. The argument to counteract such tendency in the case of individuals is that pro-environmental behaviours provide well-being in themselves, regardless of their effectiveness, in particular through a rediscovered appreciation of the natural environment and of social cooperation (see, e.g., Latouche 2008).

This approach has a fundamental weakness. While pro-environmental behaviours in production and consumption involve costs with certainty, at least in terms of time,[4] appreciating the natural environment and cooperation is an uncertain and delayed benefit. Therefore, the problem of free riding re-emerges. This brings back the standard environmentalist policies based on incentives and sanctions, which, however, have some heavy drawbacks, such as the instillation of the idea of having the right to pollute (Bolderdijk & Steg 2015).

Going beyond these approaches that already go 'beyond GDP' implies building on their strengths and alleviating their weaknesses. To this aim, we put forward a new concept of human development.

2.2   Human development as an expansion of the fundamental human capability

'Human development' is not a new notion in the study of economic growth and development of countries. Its most well-known use is attached to the mentioned UNDP's *Reports*, which is based on Amartya Sen's capability approach. According to Sen, people's advantage and freedom (rather than well-being) do not simply come from material resources but also from their capabilities to use them. Income and goods are only means, so policies should not only be concerned with growth of GDP but also with improving people's capabilities to effectively enjoy opportunities that they value and have reason to value (Sen 1999). 'Human development' is thus the term to indicate this expansion of people's capabilities.

But Sen did not define what the relevant capabilities are, so various authors have proposed their own lists. For example, the philosopher Martha Nussbaum has proposed, on the basis of insight and abstract thinking, a list of central human capabilities (Nussbaum 2010), which have been then measured with proxies, such as the health and education measures of the UNDP *Reports*. Over time, the list has tended to lengthen the number of items, thus increasing the problems of ranking them, and of assessing their weights and their reciprocal substitutability degree in order to recommend efficient policies (see, e.g., Alkire 2013; Skidelsky & Skidelsky 2013).

This book aims to solve the problem of defining the proper list of the relevant capabilities by moving from normative to interpretative purposes and by taking a very long-run perspective of past human development. The perspective will be of so long run in the past as to identify the *fundamental human capability*, meaning that which provides the foundation for other capabilities and which, taken together, have enabled human beings to improve social and material conditions and to be happy for what they have achieved. Human development cannot take place in both children and adults, in both individuals and countries, in both less and more advanced economies without the expansion of such fundamental human capability. From here on in the book, *by 'fundamental human development' we refer to the process in which humans develop their abilities to the extent that they develop their fundamental capability.* Equipped in this way, we will be able to study the effects of growth of market economies on 'fundamental human development' and hence on people's well-being. Moving from the interpretative to the normative setting, the implied recommendation will be to prioritise '(fundamental) human development', thus shaping economic growth as a powerful means for it, while considering well-being as a desirable long-run outcome.

To identify the fundamental human capability, we adopt a criterion grounded in human evolution, as studied by various disciplines. The criterion refers to what distinguishes humans from other animals. Preliminarily, by looking at how humans have populated every corner of the planet and how they have changed the environment to a level incomparable to any other animal and by observing that our success is obviously not the result of our physical abilities, we can safely say that humans are typically distinguished by *mental* capabilities, although also physical capabilities can be involved.

In the light of abundant scientific evidence, as reported below, we propose a single but twofold fundamental human capability, which we call *creativity-and-sociality*. This is a single capability because human creativity degenerates without sociality, and human sociality degenerates without creativity.

By *creativity*, we mean the ability to create new mental representations, which enable individuals to conceive goals to pursue and which help others create their own representations. Exercising this ability changes the relationship with others, and in realising the goals, it can change the material world. Creativity shapes the personal identity of individuals and the social identity of groups. In more economic terms, we can say that the individuals spend time learning from others knowledge with which to produce new options that others may find useful to increase their own options. By doing so, people accumulate their individual and collective stock of knowledge. In practice, the exercise of creativity ranges from solving ordinary open problems to innovations and artworks.[5]

By *sociality*, we do not simply mean caring for the needs of others and feeling like belonging to a group, since these are social aspects that are shared with other animals. We rather mean the ability to collaborate to conceive and realise common goals with others. This implies both interest in others, because of their different ideas, and reassurance to share a challenge with others. In economic terms, this collaboration is a special public good because it produces a greater outcome than the sum of the individual contributions and because the participants *enjoy* contributing.[6] Furthermore, since exercising sociality in this way builds on the outcomes of previous similar experiences, then participants' collaboration implies producing, consuming, and *investing* at the same time.

Creativity without sociality degenerates into conceiving or building useless or even perverse ideas and things. Perversion takes place when ideas and things become self-harming or harmful to others. Sociality without creativity degenerates into conformism to the behaviours and beliefs of the reference group. A consequence is that cohabitation of different groups in the same territory is at risk of conflict (see, e.g., Sen 2006).

Therefore, creativity and sociality must be combined to give rise to a process in which this twofold capability develops by self-generation,[7] thus forming the engine of human development. Such development mainly takes place in the first part of individuals' lives as an *internality*, that is, without much intentional planning, with the effect of changing individuals' preferences and beliefs and of increasing other abilities. In individuals' adulthood, such development mainly takes place as an *externality* across them, with the effect of improving the utilisation of social and material resources for a better quality of life.

Identifying creativity-and-sociality and hence fundamental human development as a priority in individual choices and government policy has a number of advantages over the mentioned approaches that go 'beyond GDP'. First, thus selecting a capability as fundamental and with self-dynamic property can guide the evaluation of other abilities and indices used in measuring human development. Second, people learn to prefer what makes more satisfied with themselves by learning to form and pursue their own goals rather than be attracted to the comfort as promised by the product market. This helps prevent harmful habits and addictions and suggests which market products are desirable for well-being. Third, determinants of subjective well-being can have a theoretical explanation, and more accurate indices of well-being can be devised. Fourth, prioritising creativity-and-sociality requires respecting the natural environment rather than the other way around, and it makes monetary sanctions and social approval less necessary to encourage pro-environmental behaviours.

The scientific evidence supporting the capability of creativity-and-sociality as what distinguishes humans from other animals is various. We thus conclude this section by mentioning the results of a research in comparative psychology. The next section will briefly describe the evolutionary origin of creativity-and-sociality and then the emergence in humans' birth and infancy of such capability.

A research in psychology that compares humans with other animals reviews the distinctive human abilities that are most frequently addressed and concludes that two of them are the most original and underlying all the others (Suddendorf 2013, Suddendorf et al. 2018; Bulley et al. 2020). They are:

- the ability to imagine counter-factual scenarios in a way to nest them, relate them to the unfolding events and thus to anticipate outcomes;
- the ability to share these thoughts with other human beings in a way to collectively build something that is ever greater over time.

These two abilities fit well creativity-and-sociality as we have defined it.

The other distinctive human abilities reviewed in such comparative psychology research are language, the ability to travel through time, theory of mind (i.e., the ability to understand what others think), intelligence, culture, and morality. It has thus been argued that the two identified abilities to imagine and to collaborate are necessary pre-requisites for these other abilities. Let us see briefly why in their turn.

Language can develop to communicate a thought generated by the imagination and therefore to find a correspondence and a comparison with the thought of others. This implies a confirmation for the individual of belonging to the same species with the same ability to imagine. Instead, animals communicate under the stimulus of reproduction, hunger, or fear or to control the territory. The *ability to travel through time* can be developed to predict the future by using episodes lived in the past or learned from others. Animals have no episodic memory, they cannot predict long distant future, and they are unable to imagine needs that they are not experiencing at that moment. When they store food for the winter, for example, they don't know why they do it. The *theory of mind* can be developed by using the ability to travel through time because, similarly, we can travel by reflecting on others as we reflect on ourselves. By contrast, animals like chimpanzees are only able to make connections between observed behaviours and hardly understand that others have different ideas from their own about the same event. *Intelligence*, that is the ability to understand complex concepts, to identify causality, and to solve problems, develops by decontextualising one's own and others' perceived experience to imagine new concepts. Animals are able to link in associative way between no more than three concepts at a time. *Culture* is human because only we know how to accumulate knowledge through learning from others about abstract problems, their possible solutions, and the procedures to arrive at the solution. This qualifies the kind of cooperation humans have, far beyond cooperation observed in ants or in dogs in favour of their puppies (Tomasello 2011; Lieberman 2013). Finally, *morality* develops in human beings by going beyond the compassion and mutual help that there can be among other animals. This is possible due to the human ability to reconstruct past events that allow us to understand the responsibilities in the context of the contingent culture.

2.3 The fundamental human capability in both human evolution and infancy

Creativity-and-sociality is a capability that has a clear evolutionary origin in the human species. As is well known, a mythical phase of our origin was that of coming down as great apes from the trees, a consequence of the cooling and drying of the soil that transformed the African rainforests into savannas. The new habitat exposed these apes to the danger of becoming prey for large carnivorous animals, forcing them to form groups to defend themselves and then to find new food by hunting large mammals. The new social dimension for the apes is more extensive and organisationally more complex. This is certainly not the first time that animal species have organised into large groups to survive new environmental conditions, but this time it happened to mammals with an evolved brain for memorisation and processing. Such brain is so evolved that it triggers a virtuous process: the more complex social relations become, the more the relative size of the brain grows or, more specifically, of those parts of the brain responsible for processing social complexity.[8]

The origin of our sociality dates back in the formation of large cooperative groups, which can obtain a result greater than the sum of the results that would have been obtained individually. But such cooperation has the serious problem of opportunism, that is, the individual convenience not to contribute to the group while earning the dividend obtained from the cooperation of others. The problem is serious because opportunism has a tendency to contagion, with the result of eliminating cooperation and breaking up the group. How could such an important feature of sociality have come down to us if opportunism is so insidious?

A first hypothesis to answer this question addresses punishment. According to some economists – in a first phase of prehistoric times, when the groups were still relatively small, opportunistic behaviours were punished in various ways, even if punishing was effortful. In a second phase, natural selection would have rewarded the most cooperative groups, so that human beings have generally and spontaneously become cooperative (Bowles & Gintis 2013).

Another hypothesis is based on 'partner choice' (Baumard et al. 2013; Sylwester & Roberts 2013; Barclay & Raihani 2016). In this case, cooperation takes place through experience and information, which enable the individual to choose the right partner to cooperate with. The 'partner' can then become the group or gender of people to choose. Once the interaction takes place on the basis of interest and creative exchange, individuals reveal themselves and in turn learn to choose the proper partner, so that the groups evolve and continuously recompose themselves over time. Thereby, the groups that are more cooperative will prevail, not simply because they will be able to obtain more resources for survival thanks to cooperation but also because they are able to overcome passive adaptation to the environment thanks to creative changes.[9]

A distinctive hypothesis about the origin of creativity in human beings is that of 'pretend play' typical of children, who were half of the population of that time (Picciuto & Carruthers 2013; Nowell 2015). Once the brain had increased in size and the anatomical and neuronal substrate necessary for language had also evolved, pretend play was able to exploit these possibilities. Specifically, it was able to transform the normal playful activity of children with their parents into a truly creative act through imitation, interaction, and random novelties. The commitment to play, combined with the well-being of social interaction, may have exploited the new possibilities of remembering lived episodes, of elaborating different associations, of finding new meanings, and of communicating these 'novelties' to others. The transmission and development of these skills would then take place through culture.[10]

This hypothesis fits well with the fact that sociality and the brain developed together in human beings, but it also adds an original indication: that creativity arises first among human relationships, as a general lifestyle, and then becomes the ability to invent useful tools for survival and material well-being, which is the prerogative of a few, and applied to specific problems (Burkart et al. 2009).

Our argument that creativity-and-sociality is the fundamental human capability is also supported by scientific evidence that looks at the early development of human beings as individuals (ontogenetic perspective) rather than as a species (phylogenetic perspective). This perspective allows us to observe original human abilities because they are not yet much influenced by adults.

The fact that young children already have the creativity to imagine counterfactual scenarios, even in a surprisingly elaborate way, has been recently well-recognised. By observing children under the age of 1 year in the laboratory, they seem to already know how to adopt a method quite similar to that of scientists: they first formulate a hypothesis, verify it even with observation alone, and eventually correct it if contradicted by the facts. In this way, when at the age of 1 year, they undertake to solve problems, they know how to anticipate the solution without necessarily resorting to the method of trial and error, which is instead the one used by the most intelligent animals. The ability to generate counter-factual hypotheses in the 'pretend play' helps to interpret the causality between phenomena, to predict them, and to modify their consequences. When children indulge in their fantasies, they are surprisingly concentrated and gratified, even knowing that reality is different (Gopnik et al. 2000; Gopnik 2009).

Sociality is not less elaborated in young children. In fact, they show, from an early age, to have the ability of relating with other human beings that is spontaneous, specific, affective, and cooperative. For example, some experiments have shown that 10-month-old babies already know how to distinguish people from animals and things based on their properties, as if they belonged to three different categories. This distinction also prevails over that between people (Bonatti et al. 2002).

At 12 months, children have already understood that cooperation between people goes beyond mere material opportunity because it is also a way to directly enter into relationship with others and to relate fairly with them. For example, children indicate to an adult the object they want even if they can take it, while chimpanzees indicate the object only when they cannot take it (van der goot et al. 2014). When material goods should be shared among individuals, laboratory experiments makes evident that 1.5-year-old children prefer to receive a toy from people they have seen behaving fairly (Lucca et al. 2018). When they are 8 years old, they are also able to refuse a desirable candy if it generates inequity compared with other children (McAuliffe et al. 2017; Shaw et al. 2014).

A fascinating hypothesis further explains why at birth the first capability is precisely creativity-and-sociality. According to this hypothesis, at birth, the foetus, developed in a state of homeostasis in the uterus, undergoes the shock of light, which, through the retina, activates brain functions. More precisely, the baby has a complex reaction against this shock: s/he makes the new reality disappear in her/his mind, and by drawing on the previous experience of contact with amniotic fluid, s/he activates vitality and feels the sensation of her/his existence. The intrauterine experience is also the trace that gives the baby the certainty of the existence of other human beings to relate to. Therefore, the creativity of the baby at birth lies in the ability to imagine what s/he is not yet seeing, and sociality emerges as ability to naturally recognise others as human beings.[11]

The peculiarity of the birth of human beings compared with other animals could be traced back to the insufficient maturity of the foetus to deal with the natural environment, so that babies require long care before they can survive independently. Such a 'premature' birth could be due, in turn, to the limit of the mother's physical ability to give birth to a baby with such a large brain.[12]

2.4   Human development as a self-generating process

By playing, the child does three things at the same time: s/he exercises his fundamental human capability of creativity-and-sociality, s/he increases it, and s/he feels well. When the play ends, it leaves an outcome in the child's life that could be permanent: the improvement in the capability, which can be used later for plays and other more complex activities. If at each stage of development, the child can find the right play, this fuels a virtuous cumulative process.

This is the property of self-generating development, which is extraordinary because it not only uses but also generates resources, such as the increase of the abilities and the motivation to exercise them. In fact, the child likes to play in itself well beyond the outcome of the play. This is why her/his motivation to play is called 'intrinsic'.

When the child becomes an adult and goes to work, s/he has the important goal of earning to exchange with what is necessary for subsistence. In this case, work is an instrumental activity, and the underlying motivation is called 'extrinsic'.[13]

Work can also be interesting in itself because it can have a creative component, such as resolving new problems, while being recognised by colleagues and others.[14] Similarly, leisure time can be used not only to rest and enjoy the comfort of material goods but also to learn new things and exchange ideas with others. Therefore, creativity-and-sociality can develop because work and leisure become similar to children's play, the difference being the social dimension, which, especially at work, becomes broader, and demands for greater responsibility.

Moreover, exercising our fundamental human capability as adults can add a further outcome: a new idea or even an innovation, both of which can be useful to many others. In this case, the satisfaction for having achieved the desired result is added to the excitement during the activity pursued to achieve it. In other words, extrinsic and intrinsic motivations go together. In human development as we have defined it, everything is thus inextricably intertwined. In fact, if the goal were systematically missed, the activity to achieve it would lose interest. If only the goal became important, the activity would fall back becoming instrumental, such as working only for pay.

We can thus recapitulate the process of human development of a person as a continuous transformation of inputs into outputs, where the inputs include person's initial capability of creativity-and-sociality; time and external resources, like market goods; and others' capabilities and time. The outputs are three: an increase of person's creativity-and-sociality; her/his well-being; and, possibly, new and useful knowledge and things for others.

A person's human development can be compromised if s/he encounters serious social or material adverse conditions, such as economic conditions below the subsistence level. This is especially true if it occurs in the very first part of person's life, the typical example being an inadequate caregiver.

The transformation of inputs into outputs is a process that needs time because it means exercising the fundamental human capability. Its creativity component implies that such transformation entails an uncertain outcome, thus challenging person's initial capability.[15] To be successful, s/he will search for the activities (and their complexity degree) that best match her/his fundamental human capability and that can be concretely exercised through specific skills. S/he will attempt to avoid too complex activities not to turn excitement into anxiety, while an excessively simple activity would be unattractive because it is boring.

Human development is thus a learning experience that enables the person to improve his/her human capability.[16] It is a self-generating process because improved capability provides a better input to the performance of more challenging activities, and the expected satisfaction from doing this provides the proper (intrinsic) motivation. Time and effort are no longer considered simply as costs for the person, and the development of his/her capability goes together with new relationships with others and possibly useful innovations for everybody.

We can therefore identify the goal to maximise human development in finding the best match between person's fundamental human capability and the complexity of the activities that s/he can choose to undertake, thus making the maximum possible subjective challenge successful. This is a sensible conceptual result because it offers guidance for the choices of individuals and of communities. In fact, the individuals are called to discover and know their talents, dispositions, and abilities and to explore the available options to learn the most suitable match and hence the choice that is best for them. Communities can enjoy the synergy among individuals' human development.[17]

Human development as an expansion of creativity-and-sociality may appear restricted to children and exceptional among adults, at least because people's lives appear dominated by material constraints and economic incentives. Studying with passion and working for intrinsic satisfaction are often considered additional aspects, even when economic conditions are already well above the threshold of subsistence. The frequent justification for this belief is that the different approaches to work and, more generally, to life are due to people's personality traits, which would be innate and would remain substantially unchanged throughout life or at least during adulthood. However, studies in neurobiology inform us that the brain is extremely plastic in infancy and remains plastic also in adulthood (Alos-Ferrer 2018; Davidson 2013). Studies in both psychology and economics consistently show that cognitive and socio-emotional skills definitely change, especially in childhood, and that personality traits, such as openness to experience, conscientiousness, and sociality, do change in adolescence and in adulthood.[18] Moreover, the greater stability of personality traits in adulthood may be more due to people's adoption of routines and behavioural habits than to biology (see Chernyshenko et al. 2018, and citations therein).

The role of parenting and education is undoubtedly fundamental in the formation of children's personality and skills, over and above genes (Hanushek et al. 2021). For example, the transmission from parents to children of the willingness to trust others seems more due to the environment than to direct transmission (Giulietti et al. 2016). The transmission of the attachment style (which concerns the bond with the caregiver in childhood), whether secure and autonomous or anxious and avoidant, has been observed in psychological studies (Raby et al. 2015; Mikulincer & Shaver 2007). In sociology and economics, it has been observed that strong family ties reduce trust in others (Banfield 1958; Ermisch & Gambetta 2010; Pugno 2015).

2.5   The path from human development to well-being

A frequent guess is that explaining happiness is simple because it would suffice to resort to satisfying people's desires, from the most urgent to the most delicious ones. Liberals defend the freedom of individuals to pursue any of their desires, as long as it does not harm the freedom of others. Economics textbooks represent people's behaviours as aimed at maximising their individual utility by acquiring any available means according to their preferences. Therefore, economic growth in the advanced countries would seem sufficient to provide such means to people once property rights are guaranteed. However, our approach to human development rather tells a somewhat different story.

The ancient Greek philosophers distinguished between two different paths to happiness. The pursuit of pleasure as a good feeling is the path to happiness that was called 'hedonism'. Exercising skills as dispositions that enable the persons to accomplish activities in an excellent way is the path to happiness called 'eudaimonia' (Keyes & Annas 2009; Pugno 2021). This distinction will help us understand how economic growth and human development can distinctly bring well-being to people. Indeed, recent field and laboratory investigations have rediscovered the two paths to well-being.

Psychological studies provide the first evidence. In a number of surveys, people were asked to indicate their preferences within a predetermined list of sensations and self-assessments. People thus significantly polarised into two groups. One group especially appreciated pleasure and comfort; the other group preferred to feel a meaning and a value in what they did, to take an interest in new things, to feel competent and capable of having good relationships (Huta 2015). When a survey presented a list focused on relationships with others only, the following polarisation emerged. One group thought it is mostly important to 'feel accepted' and 'fear of being alone'; the other group considered it is mostly important to 'exchange ideas' and to 'discover many things about others and about themselves' (Lavigne et al. 2011).

The distinction between the two paths to well-being can be reformulated in the following more precise terms. In the first path, people aim to achieve pleasure and comfort, including social comfort, by buying market products (and social approval) in exchange of income and ultimately of work and effort. The motivation to work and possibly to study for a better job is extrinsic because it is directed on the means to achieve well-being as the final end. In the second path to well-being, people challenge their skills by using adequate opportunities to realise goals recognised as valuable to themselves and to others, thus achieving well-being. The underlying motivation is intrinsic because both exercising the skills and realising the goals yield well-being as a satisfying way of life.[19]

We can thus distinguish *well-being as pleasure and comfort* and *well-being in developing skills* by looking at the paths to achieve them rather than at a different subjective status.[20] In fact, moments of pleasure and comfort can be part of the well-being in developing skills.[21] Therefore, in empirical works, it is safer to distinguish the two paths to well-being by looking at the antecedents of well-being, such as the extrinsic and intrinsic motivations or the different types of skills involved.

For example, an economic study covering over 10,000 adult inhabitants of 10 advanced countries distinguished people with greater intrinsic motivations for work from those with greater extrinsic motivations. More precisely, it distinguished those who, thinking about work, placed the highest importance on the feeling of accomplishment and on the relationships on the job from those who believed that earning a good pay and having a secure job was more important. The group with mixed motivations is left aside. This study then showed that people with greater intrinsic motivations reported a higher life satisfaction independent from income, health, and social status and with higher levels for older people after near-constant levels for young and middle-aged people (Salinas-Jiménez et al. 2010).[22] This last result is consistent with the hypothesis that pursuing the accomplishment of skills tends to make people more and more satisfied with themselves, as the process of human development would predict.

Other economic studies based on laboratory experiments demonstrate causality from a measure of general human skill, which nicely captures the fundamental human capability, to different measures of well-being, including long-run happiness. The measure of general skill combines self-confidence, identifying and pursuing life goals, and establishing warm and trusting relationships with others without depending on them. These studies also demonstrate the contextual causality from this general skill to pro-social behaviours in terms of generosity, trust, and cooperation. All other reverse causalities and the causality stemming from income emerge as much weaker (Konow & Earley 2008; Koch 2016).

A number of other studies confirm or extend these results. Different psychological studies establish the links between intrinsic motivation, the threefold skill of autonomy-competence-sociality and well-being (Deci & Ryan 2000),[23] between intrinsic motivation and creativity, and between creativity and well-being (Hennessey & Amabile 2010; Flor et al. 2013; Conner et al. 2018).[24] A strong link is also found between a general human skill (capturing self-esteem, the pursuit of life goals, and good relationships) and objective indicators of physical health detected in the laboratory, such as immune biomarkers (Keyes et al. 2002; Ryff et al. 2004; Ryff 2014).

Therefore, all these empirical results encourage us to identify a path to well-being derived from exercising the capability of creativity-and-sociality, that is, from human development, as distinct from the path going from economic growth to well-being as pleasure and comfort. The former also emerges as a more effective path because endowed with the self-generating property of creativity-and-sociality, while the latter is completely dependent on the inputs produced by the market.

2.6 Ill-beings from weak human development

Well-being and ill-being are not symmetrical, as argued in positive psychology (Seligman & Csikszentmihalyi 2000). In this section, we thus move a step forward by showing how a weak human development is specifically linked to ill-being. In this way, we can describe behaviours and malaise that are frequently observable even in the advanced economies and introduce the issue of why economic growth can deteriorate people's well-being and social cohesion.

As human development arises from the interaction between creativity and sociality, we can distinguish two main channels going from a weak human development to ill-being: the channel where behaviours are weak in sociality and the channel where behaviours are apparently strong in sociality but weak in creativity. In this description, two well-known caricatures will help us: *Homo economicus* and *Homo sociologicus*.

Homo economicus as depicted in economics textbooks is a useful caricature for describing behaviours with weak sociality, as he looks to his own interests rather than the well-being of others. To maximise his own utility, *Homo economicus* adopts the opportunistic logic of the market, in which relationships among people are governed by competition in finding the most convenient exchange of things and services. To keep this cost–benefit accounting and thus calculate the convenience of the exchange, he uses rationality. Therefore, *Homo economicus* considers people only instrumentally as a rational opportunity for his own convenience in exchanges, and, in the long run, in the division of labour and in the specialisation of production. Even when he spends time learning, the goal is to have more command on material resources in the future.

Considering the relationship with others as end in itself, as required by human development, does not fall within the horizon of *Homo economicus*. For example, parents' altruism towards their children becomes for *Homo economicus* an investment of resources such as time and goods in exchange with a future return when he becomes elderly and needs help (Becker et al. 2016). American families appear to be generous because they donate an average of $1,600 per year, but several studies have shown, with both experimental and field analyses, that an important reason for making donations is to have social visibility in return (Ariely et al. 2009).

Homo economicus is thus not genuinely generous and generally does not trust others, like strangers. But this turns against him because the lack of generosity and general trust brings ill-being, as demonstrated by amount of evidence in different disciplines. For example, according to a recent economic study, lower levels of general trust are associated with less subjective well-being, less resilience to adverse shocks, and less cooperation, in terms of charitable activities, voting frequency, and pro-environmental behaviours (Carattini & Roesti 2020).[25] Two other studies in economics and, respectively, psychology show that less general trust significantly predicts more suicides and higher mortality rates (Helliwell 2007; Barefoot et al. 1998).

But the opportunistic behaviour of *Homo economicus* is not a completely false representation of the behaviour of ordinary people because external circumstances can induce people to resemble *Homo economicus*. A frequent circumstance is the others' defection to contribute to public goods, which is a powerful trigger for the contagion of opportunistic behaviour (Fehr & Gaechter 2000). Another case studied in the experimental setting reveals that people may *learn* dishonest behaviour when its monetary convenience increases from low levels (Mazar et al. 2006; Welsh et al. 2015).[26] Therefore, people lacking in sociality to prioritise self-interest not only may experience reduced well-being but may also even have learned self-interested behaviours in the expectation of improving their own well-being.

Other people' behaviours that rather prioritise sociality seem also frequent and may appear as an effective barrier to pervading opportunistic behaviours. However, we should recognise that social behaviour may be weak in creativity in such case and that it may still bring ill-being. To discuss this case, we refer to the caricature of *Homo sociologicus* as an easy and somewhat ironic symmetry with the other *Homo*.

Homo sociologicus is useful for representing conformist behaviours, meaning the tendency to imitate others or, more precisely, to come closer to the behaviours that others expect according to social norms. Social norms differ among social groups in history and tradition, so that the conformist behaviours of a single person at a certain time should refer to a specific group (Subrt 2015; Tajfel & Turner 1979).[27] The behaviours of *Homo sociologicus* require constant comparison with others and thus tend to be repetitive. Novel behaviours are at risk of social disapproval and rejection, and this discourages looking with interest at differences with others to form one's own ideas and goals. Indeed, the expected benefit of conformism is due to the approval from others, the feeling of belonging to the group, or even the identification with the group. *Homo sociologicus* thus exhibits social behaviours but lacks creativity, that is, to imagine and pursue an original autonomous behaviour.[28]

Three negative consequences follow. First, systematic comparison with others devalues the psychological and material resources that people already have. This reduces the well-being that could alternatively be enjoyed for the progress made with respect to the past or for the opportunities suggested by the example of others. An amount of evidence confirms that the comparison with the income of others can heavily deflate the enjoyment of one's own income. In particular, it has been observed that the greater the importance attributed to this comparison, the lower the subjective well-being (Easterlin 1995; Proto & Rustichini 2013; Clark & Senik 2010; Budria & Ferre-I-Carbonell 2019). The second consequence is that failing to exercise autonomy strengthens people's belief that the course of their lives is due to external forces, namely in psychology terms, that their 'locus of control' is external (Rotter 1966; Kormanik & Rocco 2009). Again, economic studies show that people with an external locus of control enjoy less subjective well-being and are less resilient to adverse shocks (Verme 2009; Buddelmeyer & Powdthavee 2016).

The third negative consequence of the conformist behaviour is the consolidation of groups including similar individuals with their own norms and distinctive characters, that is, with their own social identity. As the deviation from the norms is disapproved, contiguity between groups gives likely rise to distrust, competition, friction, and, possibly, conflict. Examples of such close-knit groups are gangs and mafia organisations and even families when the ties are especially exclusive.[29] Looking at the recent United States, exclusive and intransigent communities are strengthening on the basis of the same political conviction, with consequent increasing social frictions (see Chapter 1).

We cannot deny that both (instrumental) rationality and social norms are necessary for human development, although they are also used by *Homo economicus* and *Homo sociologicus*, respectively. But in human development, rationality is used in the creative process along with so-called 'divergent thinking'. This type of thinking is characterised by widespread attention, intuition, and imagination and is at the basis of the generation of novelties, which can open new possibilities of choice.[30] Rationality is necessary at the beginning, in the search and selection of the interesting elements for divergent thinking, and afterwards, in the evaluation of the novelties with respect to the existing choices. Social norms are also necessary at the beginning, as they provide stable ground conditions and govern the direction of action and research, and afterwards, as they provide criteria for evaluating novelties. If the novelties are validated, the social norms undergo a change, and the old ones are overcome.[31]

Analogously, living in groups is helpful for human development but only when enriched with creativity. The most basic case is the family, as the group in which children develop in protected environment to acquire the necessary security to build new relationships with strangers. The most sophisticated case is the scientific research groups such as that of CERN (European Organization for Nuclear Research), which attracts researchers from all over the world with the sole purpose of increasing scientific knowledge. At the opposite, when groups are conservative, such as groups based on obedience to traditions, and groups based on particular interests, also called Olson groups, then human development tends to weaken (Degli Antoni & Grimalda 2016; Bartolini et al. 2013). For example, when obedience is the quality that children are mostly encouraged to learn at home, people report feeling less accomplished from what they do, learning fewer things in life, taking less care of others, and feeling less cared for by others – according to a study based on an European sample of countries (Conzo et al. 2017).

Notes

1 This approach is much indebted to Amartya Sen and Martha Nussbaum's work (see Alkire 2010).
2 As an illustrative example, the percentage of deaths in the US due to a lifestyle that does not comply with the prescriptions on risk factors, such as tobacco smoking, poor diet, physical inactivity, and alcohol intake, was estimated at 50% both in 1990 and in 2000 (Mokdad et al. 2004).
3 A discussion on the limits of the life satisfaction measure is provided by Pugno (2016) and the literature cited therein. Rojas (2007) shows how different are the conceptual reference when people say that they are happy or not.
4 Binder & Blankenberg (2017) show that pro-environmental consumer behaviours have negative effects on subjective well-being if the self-image of being environmentally friendly is taken into account.
5 Geniuses' sociality is evident in their intrinsically humanity-oriented thought.
6 See the discussion and formalisations of these goods, called 'relational goods', in Uhlaner (1989), Gui & Sugden (2005), Pugno (2009).
7 In this way, the weakness of the capability approach to be static can be overcome. See Heckman & Corbin (2016) and Pugno (2017).
8 Dunbar & Shultz (2007) show that the numerosity of groups in which different primate species live predicts the relative size of the neocortex of their brains.
9 This explanation of the origin of cooperation among people based on interest in the ideas of others and on creativity has the advantages, on the one hand, of maintaining an 'opportunist' aspect and, on the other, of not having to resort to a

pure altruistic motivation (Tomasello et al. 2012). It has the further advantage of helping to explain, through the appreciation of the abilities of others, the origin of the sense of equity and morality (Baumard et al. 2013).

10 According to several researchers, Darwin's evolutionary approach, although updated with recent discoveries such as those on character inheritance, is not sufficient to explain the origin of the human species (Gabora & Kaufman 2010). Although some economists also consider the Darwinian approach to be sufficient (Hodgson & Knudsen 2006; Rayo & Becker 2007), an alternative approach inspired by Lamarck is emerging. According to this approach, the evolution, instead of taking place through the selection of random variants, would have occurred through the modeling of images in the relationship with reality (Gabora & Kaufman 2010; for a review on the contrast between the two approaches from an economic viewpoint, see Frigotto 2018).

11 Fagioli (2019). For supporting evidence, see Gatti et al. (2012), Polli et al. (2010), Vandewalle et al. (2013), and Tinsely et al. (2016).

12 Some calculation shows that the required months of gestation should be 18–21 months, instead of 9, for the baby to be born at a stage of neurological development equivalent to that of the newborn chimpanzee (Dunsworth et al. 2012). See also Roberts & Thorpe (2014).

13 According to Deci & Ryan (2000:233) – "Intrinsically motivated behaviors are those that are freely engaged out of interest without the necessity of separable consequences", while the goal of 'extrinsic motivations' are precisely the "separable consequences". See also the economists Scitovsky (1986) and Frey (1997).

14 The job characteristics related to intrinsic motivation are the 'skill variety' required by the tasks performed; 'task identity' as attached to an identifiable piece of work; the 'task significance', as derived from the impact on the lives of others; 'autonomy', as it provides freedom, independence, and discretion; and 'feedback from work' on the effectiveness of the tasks performed (Kuvaas 2018).

15 This is a strong form of uncertainty because the person cannot know the distribution of probability of success of his undertaking (see, e.g., Dequech 2000). In the case of challenging activities, the undertaking cannot be repeated without changing person's skills and hence the premises for further action.

16 The fact that learning requires time is confirmed by neurobiologists because it entails special internal changes of the human body (Immordino-Yang 2016).

17 This dynamics is represented in a formal model by Pugno (2013) and more extensively by Pugno (2016). The model is developed on the basis of the insights of an economist and a psychologist, Tibor Scitovsky (1976) and Mihalyi Csikszentmihalyi (1990), respectively.

18 See the studies by psychologists Elkins et al. (2017), Roberts et al. (2006), and Specht et al. (2014), as well as the systematisation of the matter in economic terms by Almlund et al. (2011). An example of an economic study is by Boyce et al. (2013), which shows that the variability of personality traits during the adult lives of people is similar to the variability of their income and is even more important in influencing their life satisfaction.

19 Some psychological researchers argue that the well-being obtained from pursuing a goal may be even greater than its achievement (Klug & Maier 2015; Kaftan & Freund 2018). Others observe that intrinsic motivations are to be especially effective when the tasks are complex and creative (Camerer & Hogarth 1999; Amabile & Pillemer 2012).

20 Some measures refer to momentary feelings and affect for the first type of well-being and to meaning and purpose of life for the second type. Clark &

Senik (2011) find little difference by looking at the correlates of the two types of well-being, thus implicitly suggesting that life satisfaction be referred to as a synthetic measure of well-being.

21 Instead, when the pursuit of well-being as pleasure and comfort requires some specific skills, these are minimised because they are considered only effortful (Huta & Waterman 2014).

22 Another study that focuses on the years immediately preceding people's deaths shows that well-being declines less if people are engaged in cultural and social activities and if they attach importance to pro-social activities (Gerstorf et al. 2016).

23 For an economic interpretation of Deci and Ryan theory of motivations, see Pugno (2008b, 2011).

24 The link between creativity and well-being in geniuses is another more complex matter (see, e.g., Simonton 2010).

25 See confirmation in Helliwell et al. (2016). For evidence on how much self-declared trust predicts actual behaviours, see Farina et al. (2009).

26 This escalation towards dishonesty – according to a study in neuroscience – also has a correlation in neurological adaptation (Garrett et al. 2016). Bowles (2016) provides many other examples of how incentives make people selfish.

27 For an economic reformulation of conformism, see Bernheim (1994).

28 The sociologist Raymond Boudon recognises that the *Homo sociologicus* thus defined is an 'irrational idiot' because it renounces his freedom of choice. He therefore suggests re-defining it by taking into account the rationality of *Homo economicus*, though he still considers it insufficient (Boudon 2006).

29 This problem is recognised by Amartya Sen in the book with the telling title *Identity and violence* (Sen 2006). For the issue of social identity, see Akerlof & Kranton (2000, 2010).

30 Sowden et al. (2015).

31 Human beings obviously have a limited rationality (Simon 1955), make logical errors, and use heuristics (Kahneman 2003; Thaler 2000), but this does not imply that, for their development, they must strive for unlimited rationality. For example, in the presence of bounded rationality, social norms can help make the most beneficial decisions in the long run when interacting with others (Axelrod 1986).

References

Akerlof GA, Kranton RE (2000) Economics and identity. *Quarterly Journal of Economics* 115(3):715–753

Akerlof GA, Kranton RE (2010) *Identity Economics*. Princeton: Princeton University Press

Alkire S (2010) Human development: Definitions, critiques, and related concepts. *UNDP Research Paper*, June 2010/1, https://www.ophi.org.uk/wp-content/uploads/OPHI_WP36.pdf

Almlund M, Duckworth AL, Heckman JJ, Kautz TD (2011) Personality psychology and economics. In EA Hanushek, S Machin, L Woessmann (eds) *Handbook of Economics of Education*. Amsterdam: Elsevier, pp. 1–181

Alos-Ferrer C (2018) A review essay on Social Neuroscience. *Journal of Economic Literature* 56:234–264

Amabile TM, Pillemer J (2012) Perspectives on the social psychology of creativity. *Journal of Creative Behavior* 46(1):3–15

Ariely D, Bracha A, Meier S (2009) Doing good or doing well? *American Economic Review* 99:544–555

Axelrod R (1986) An evolutionary approach to norms. *American Political Science Review* 80:1095–1111

Bachelet M, Becchetti L, Pisani F (2020) Eudaimonic happiness as a leading health indicator. *Applied Economics* 52:4726–4744

Banfield EC (1958) *The Moral Basis of a Backward Society*. Free Press, New York

Barclay P, Raihani N (2016) Partner choice versus punishment in human Prisoner's Dilemmas. *Evolution and Human Behavior* 37:263–271

Barefoot JC, Maynard KE, Beckham JC, Brummett BH, Hooker K, Siegler IC (1998) Trust, health, and longevity. *Journal of Behavioral Medicine* 21:517–626

Bartolini S, Bilancini E, Pugno M (2013) Did the decline in social connections depress Americans' happiness. *Social Indicators Research* 110(3):1033–1059

Baumard N, André J-B, Sperber D (2013) A mutualistic approach to morality. *Behavioral and Brain Science* 36:59–122

Becker GS, Murphy KM, Spenkuch JL (2016) The manipulation of children's preferences, old age support, and investment in children's human capital. *Journal of Labor Economics* 34:S3–S30

Bernheim BD (1994) A theory of conformity. *Journal of Political Economy* 102:841–877

Binder M, Blankenberg A-K (2017) Green lifestyles and subjective well-being. *Journal of Economic Behavior & Organization* 137:304–323

Bolderdijk JW, Steg L (2015) Promoting sustainable consumption: The risks of using financial incentives. In LA Reisch, J Thøgersen (eds) *Handbook of Research on Sustainable Consumption*. Cheltenham: Elgar, pp. 328–342

Bonatti L, Frot E, Zangl R, Mehler J (2002) The human first hypothesis. *Cognitive Psychology* 44:388–426

Boudon R (2006) Are we doomed to see the *homo sociologicus* as a rational or as an irrational idiot? In J Elster, O Gjelsvik, A Hylland, K Moene (eds) *Understanding Choice, Explaining Behaviour*. Oslo: Unipub, pp. 35–42

Bowles S (2016) *The Moral Economy*. New Haven, CT: Yale University Press

Bowles S, Gintis H (2013). *A Cooperative Species*. Oxford: Oxford University Press

Boyce CL, Wood AM, Powdthavee N (2013) Is personality fixed? *Social Indicators Research* 111(1):287–305

Boyle PA, Barnes LL, Buchman AS, Bennet TA (2009) Purpose in life is associated with mortality among community-dwelling older persons. *Psychosomatic Medicine* 71:574–579

Buddelmeyer H, Powdthavee N (2016) Can having internal locus of control insure against negative shocks? *Journal of Economic Behavior & Organization* 122:88–109

Budria S, Ferrer-I-Carbonell A (2019) Life satisfaction, income comparisons and personality traits. *Review of Income and Wealth* 65:337–357

Bulley A, Redshaw J, Suddendorf T (2020) The future-directed functions of the imagination. In A Abraham (ed) *Cambridge Handbook of the Imagination*. Cambridge: Cambridge University Press, pp. 425–444

Burkart JM, Hrdy B, Van Schaik CP (2009) Cooperative breeding and human cognitive evolution. *Evolutionary Anthropology* 18:175–186

Camerer CF, Hogarth RM (1999) The effects of financial incentives in experiments. *Journal of Risk and Uncertainty* 19:7–42

Carattini S, Roesti M (2020) Trust, happiness, and pro-social behavior. *CESifo Working Paper*, No. 8562, https://www.econstor.eu/bitstream/10419/226264/1/cesifo1_wp8562.pdf

Chernyshenko O, Kankaraš M, Drasgow F (2018) Social and emotional skills for student success and wellbeing. *OECD Education Working Papers*, No.173. OECD Publishing, Paris

Clark AE, Senik C (2010) Who compares to whom? *Economic Journal* 120:573–594

Clark AE, Senik C (2011) Is happiness different from flourishing? *Revue d'économie politique* 121:17–34

Conner TS, DeYoung CG, Silvia PJ (2018) Everyday creative activity as a path to flourishing. *Journal of Positive Psychology* 13:181–189

Conzo P, Aassve A, Fuochi G, Mencarini L (2017) The cultural foundations of happiness. *Journal of Economic Psychology* 62:268–283

Csikszentmihalyi M (1990) *Flow*. London: Rider

Davidson RJ (2013) *The Emotional Life of Yor Brain*. London: Penguin

Deci EL, Ryan RM (2000) The "what" and "why" of goal pursuits. *Psychological Inquiry* 11:227–268

Degli Antoni G, Grimalda G (2016) Groups and trust. *Journal of Behavioral and Experimental Economics* 61:38–54

Dequech D (2000) Fundamental uncertainty and ambiguity. *Eastern Economic Journal* 26:41–60

Dunbar RIM, Shultz S (2007) Understanding primate brain evolution. *Philosophical Transaction of the Royal Society B* 362:649–658

Dunsworth HM, Warrener AG, Deacon T, Ellison PT, Pontzer H (2012) Metabolic hypothesis for human altriciality. *PNAS of the USA* 109:15212–15216

Easterlin RA (1995) Will raising the incomes of all increase the happiness of all? *Journal of Economic Behavior & Organization* 27(1):35–47

Elkins RK, Kassenboehmer SC, Schurer S (2017) The stability of personality traits in adolescence and young adulthood. *Journal of Economic Psychology* 60:37–52

Ermisch J, Gambetta D (2010) Do strong family ties inhibit trust? *Journal of Economic Behavior & Organization* 75(3):365–376

Fagioli M (2019) *Death Instinct and Knowledge*. Rome: L'Asino d'Oro

Farina F, O'Higgins N, Sbriglia P (2009) Suit the action to the word, the word to the action: Eliciting motives for trust and reciprocity by attitudinal and behavioural measures. *Research in Economics* 63:253–265

Fehr E, Gaechter S (2000) Fairness and retaliation. *Journal of Economic Perspectives* 14(3):159–181

Flor RK, Bita A, Monir KC (2013) The effect of teaching critical and creative thinking skills on the locus of control and psychological well-being in adolescents. *Procedia – Social and Behavioral Sciences* 82:51–56

Frey BS (1997) On the relationship between intrinsic and extrinsic work motivation. *International Journal of Industrial Organization* 15(4):427–39

Frigotto ML (2018) Novelty in evolution. In ML Frigotto (ed) *Understanding Novelty in Organizations*. Palgrave, pp. 15–52, Cham, Switzerland

Frijters P, Clark E, Krekel C, Layard R (2020) A happy choice: Wellbeing as the goal of government. *Behavioural Public Policy* 4(2):126–165

Gabora L, Kaufman S (2010) Evolutionary approaches to creativity. In J Kaufman, R Sternberg (eds) *The Cambridge Handbook of Creativity*. Cambridge: Cambridge University Press, pp. 279–300

Garrett N, Lazzaro SC, Ariely D, Sharot T (2016) The brain adapts to dishonesty. *Nature Neuroscience* 19(12):1727–1732

Gatti MG, Becucci E, Fargnoli F, Fagioli M, Ådén U, Buonocore G. (2012) Functional maturation of neocortex. *Journal of Maternal-Fetal & Neonatal Medicine* 25(1):101–103

Gerstorf D, Hoppmann CA, Löckenhoff CE, Infurna FJ (2016) Terminal decline in well-being. *Psychology and Aging* 31(2):149–165

Giulietti C, Rettore E, Tonini S (2016) The chips are down: The influence of family on children's trust formation. *IZA DP*, No. 9999, https://docs.iza.org/dp9999.pdf

Gopnik A (2009) *The Philosophical Baby*. Farrar, Straus and Giroux, New York

Gopnik A, Meltzoff AN, Kuhl PK (2000) *The Scientist in the Crib*. Harper & Collins, New York

Gui B, Sugden R (eds) (2005) *Economics and Social Interaction*. Cambridge: Cambridge University Press

Hanushek EA, Jacobs B, Schwerdt G, van der Velden R, et al. (2021) The intergenerational transmission of skills: An investigation of the causal impact of families on student outcomes. *NBER Working Paper*, No. 29450, https://www.nber.org/papers/w29450

Heckman JJ, Corbin CO (2016) Capabilities and skills. *Journal of Human Development and Capabilities* 17(3):342–359

Helliwell J (2007) Well-being and social capital: Does suicide pose a puzzle? *Social Indicators Research* 81:455–496

Helliwell JF, Huang H, Wang S (2016). New evidence on trust and wellbeing. *NBER Working Paper*, No. 22450. Cambridge, MA, https://www.nber.org/papers/w22450

Hennessey BA, Amabile TM (2010) Creativity. *Annual Review of Psychology* 61:569–598

Hodgson GM, Knudsen T (2006) Dismantling Lamarckism. *Journal of Economic Evolution* 16:343–366

Huta V, Waterman AS (2014) Eudaimonia and its distinction from hedonia. *Journal of Happiness Studies* 15:1425–1456

Huta V (2015) An overview of hedonic and eudaimonic well-being concepts. In L Reinecke, MB Oliver (eds) *Handbook of Media Use and Well-being*. New York: Routledge, pp. 14–33

Immordino-Yang MH (2016) *Emotions, Learning, and the Brain*. Norton, New York

Kaftan OJ, Freund AM (2018) The way is the goal. In E Diener, S Oishi, L Tay (eds) *Handbook of Well-being*. Salt Lake City: DEF Publishers

Kahneman D (2003) Maps of bounded rationality. *American Economic Review* 93(5):1449–1475

Keyes CLM, Annas J (2009) Feeling good and functioning well: Distinctive concepts in ancient philosophy and contemporary science. *Journal of Positive Psychology* 4:197–201

Keyes CLM, Ryff CD, Shmotkin D (2002) Optimizing well-being. *Journal of Personality and Social Psychology* 28(1007):22

Klug HJP, Maier GW (2015) Linking goal progress and subjective well-being: A meta-analysis. *Journal of Happiness Studies* 16:37–65

Koch C (2016) *Is There a Nexus Between Pro-social Behaviour and Well-being?* Available at SSRN 2584334. Retrieved [20 Feb. 2022] from: https://drive.google.com/file/d/13yXjl9XSAUah7TMeSh5cAqL8OSY0AHe0/view

Konow J, Earley J (2008) The hedonistic paradox. *Journal of Public Economics* 92(1–2):1–33

Kormanik MB, Rocco TS (2009) Internal versus external control of reinforcement. *Human Resources Development Review* 8(4):463–483

Kuvaas B (2018). The relative efficiency of extrinsic and intrinsic motivation. In A Sasson (ed) *At the Forefront, Looking Ahead Research-Based Answers to Contemporary Uncertainties of Management.* Universitetsforlaget, Oslo, pp. 198–213

Latouche S (2008) Petit Traité de la Décroissance Sereine, *Mille et Une Nuits, Paris*

Lavigne GL, Vallerand RJ, Crevier-Braud L (2011) The fundamental need to belong. *Personality and Social Psychology Bulletin* 37:1185–1201

Lieberman MD (2013) *Social: Why Our Brains Are Wired to Connect.* New York: Crown

Lucca K, Pospisil J, Sommerville JA (2018) Fairness informs social decision making in infancy. *PLoS ONE* 13(2):e0192848

Mazar N, Ariely D (2006) Dishonesty in everyday life and its policy implications. *Journal of Public Policy & Marketing* 25(1):117–126

McAuliffe K, Blake PR, Steinbeis N, Warneken F (2017) The developmental foundations of human fairness. *Nature Human Behaviour*:1–9

Mikulincer M, Shaver PR (2007) *Attachment in Adulthood.* New York: Guilford Press

Mokdad AH, Marks JS, Stroup DF, Gerberding JL (2004) Actual causes of death in the United States, 2000. *JAMA* 291(10):1238–1245

Nowell A (2015) Childhood, play and the evolution of cultural capacity in Neandertals and modern humans. In M Haidle, N Conard, M Bolus (eds) *The Nature of Culture.* Springer, Dordrecht, pp. 87–97

Nussbaum MC (2010) *Not for Profit.* Princeton: Princeton University Press

Picciuto E, Carruthers P (2013) The origins of creativity. In E Paul, S Kaufman (eds) *The Philosophy of Creativity.* Oxford: Oxford University Press

Polli D, Alto P, Weingart O et al. (2010) Conical intersection dynamics of the primary photoisomerization event in vision. *Nature* 467:440–443

Powdthavee N, Lekfuangfu WN, Wooden M (2015). What's the good of education on our overall quality of life? *Journal of Behavioral and Experimental Economics* 54:10–21

Proto E, Rustichini A (2013) A reassessment of the relationship between GDP and life satisfaction. *PLoS ONE* 8(11):e79358

Pugno M (2008a) Capabilities, the self, and well-being. In L Bruni, F Comim, M Pugno (eds) *Capabilities and Happiness*. Oxford: Oxford University Press, pp. 224–253

Pugno M (2008b) Economics and the self. A formalisation of self-determination theory. *Journal of Socio-Economics* 37:1328–1346

Pugno M (2009) The Easterlin paradox and the decline of social capital: An integrated explanation. *Journal of Socio-Economics* 38(4):590–600

Pugno M (2011) Economy, people's personal motivation and well-being. In VI Chirkov, RM Ryan, KM Sheldon (eds) *Human Autonomy in Cultural Contexts: Perspectives on the Psychology of Agency, Freedom, and Well-being*. Heidelberg: Springer, pp. 207–239

Pugno M (2013) Scitovsky and the income-happiness paradox. *Journal of Socio-Economics* 43:1–10

Pugno M (2015) Trust, family, and education. *International Journal of Happiness and Development* 2(3):216–230

Pugno M (2016) *On the Foundations of Happiness in Economics*. London: Routledge

Pugno M (2017) Scitovsky meets Sen: endogenising the dynamics of capability. *Cambridge Journal of Economics* 41(4):1177–1196

Pugno M (2021) The economics of eudaimonia. In L Bruni, A Smerilli, D De Rosa (eds) *A Modern Guide to the Economics of Happiness*. London: Elgar, pp. 46–66

Raby LK, Steele RD, Carlson EA, Sroufe LA (2015) Continuities and changes in infant attachment patters across two generations. *Attachment & Human Development* 17(4):414–428

Rayo L, Becker GS (2007) Evolutionary efficiency and happiness. *Journal of Political Economy* 115:302–337

Roberts AM, Thorpe SKS (2014). Challenges to human uniqueness. *Journal of Zoology* 292:281–289

Roberts BW, Walton KE, Viechtbauer W (2006) Patterns of mean-level change in personality traits across the life course. *Psychological Bulletin* 132:1–25

Rojas, M. (2007) Heterogeneity in the relationship between income and happiness. *Journal of Economic Psychology* 28:1–14

Rotter JB (1966) Generalized expectancies for internal versus external control of reinforcement. *Psychological Monographs* 80(1, Whole No. 609)

Ryff CD, Singer BC, Love GD (2004) Positive health: Connecting well-being with biology. *Philosophical Transactions of the Royal Society B* 359:1383–1394

Ryff CD (2014) Psychological well-being revisited. *Psychotherapy and Psychosomatics* 83:10–28

Salinas-Jiménez MdM, Artés J, Salinas-Jiménez J (2010) Income, motivation, and satisfaction with life. *Journal of Happiness Studies* 11:779–793

Scitovsky T (1976). *The Joyless Economy*. Oxford: Oxford University Press

Scitovsky T (1986) *Human Desires and Economic Satisfaction*. New York: New York University Press

Seligman MEP, Csikszentmihalyi M (2000) Positive psychology. *American Psychologist* 55(1):5–14

Sen AK (1999) *Development as Freedom*. New York: Knopf

Sen AK (2006) *Identity and Violence*. Norton, New York

Shaw A, Montinari N, Piovesan M et al (2014) Children develop a veil of fairness. *Journal of Experimental Psychology: General* 143:363–375

Skidelsky R, Skidelsky E (2013) *How Much is Enough?* London: Penguin

Simon H (1955) A behavioral model of rational choice. *Quarterly Journal of Economics* 69(1):99–118

Simonton DK (2010) So you want to become a creative genius? In DH Cropley, AJ Cropley, JC Kaufman, MA Runco (eds) *The Dark Side of Creativity.* Cambridge: Cambridge University Press, pp. 2018–2034

Sowden PT, et al. (2015) The shifting sands of creative thinking. *Thinking & Reasoning* 21:40–60

Specht J, Bleidorn W, Denissen JJA, et al (2014) What drives adult personality development? *European Journal of Personality* 28:216–230

Subrt J (2015) Homo sociologicus revisited. *Scientific Cooperations International Journal of Arts, Humanities and Social Sciences* 1(1):37–52

Suddendorf T (2013) *The Gap. The Science of What Separates us From Other Animals.* New York: Basic Books

Suddendorf T, Bulley A, Miloyan B (2018) Prospection and natural selection. *Current Opinion in Behavioral Sciences* 24:26–31

Sylwester K, Roberts G (2013) Reputation-based partner choice in an effective alternative to indirect reciprocity in solving social dilemmas. *Evolution and Human Behavior* 34:201–206

Tajfel H, Turner J (1979) An integrative theory of intergroup conflict. In W Austin, S Worchel (eds) *The Social Psychology of Intergroup Relations.* Monterey, CA: Brooks Cole

Thaler RH (2000) From Homo economicus to Homo sapiens. *Journal of Economic Perspectives* 14:133–141

Tinsely JN, Molodtsofv MI, Prevedel R, et al. (2016) Direct detection of single photon by humans. *Nature Communications* 7:12172

Tomasello M (2011) Human culture in evolutionary perspective. In MJ Gelfand, CY Chiu, Y-Y Hong (eds) *Advances in Culture and Psychology.* Oxford: Oxford University Press, pp. 5–51

Tomasello M, Melis AP, Tennie C, Wyman E, Herrmann E (2012) Two key steps in the evolution of human cooperation. *Current Anthropology* 53:673–692

Uhlaner CJ (1989) 'Relational goods' and participation. *Public Choice* 62:253–285

UNDP (1997) *Human Development Report 1997.* New York: Oxford University Press

van der goot MH, Liszkowsyi U, Tomasello M (2014) Differences in the non verbal requests of great apes and human infants. *Child Development* 85:444–455

Vandewalle G, Collignon O, Hull JT, et al. (2013) Blue light stimulates cognitive brain activity in visually blind individuals. *Journal of Cognitive Neuroscience* 25:2072–2085

Verme P (2009) Happiness, freedom and control. *Journal of Economic Behavior & Organization* 71(2):146–161

Welsh DT, Ordóñez LD, Snyder DG, Christian MS (2015). The slippery slope: How small ethical transgressions pave the way for larger future transgressions. *Journal of Applied Psychology* 100(1):114–127

3 Why growth in market economies can deteriorate human development and well-being

3.1 A new and comprehensive explanation

Economic growth in market economies comes with costs, such as cyclical instability, economic inequality, and environmental degradation. But the case of the United States (US), where the average well-being of the population has deteriorated, raises the question of whether the costs, in the long run, outweigh the benefits and whether such economic growth is able to produce greater well-being for the future.

This chapter uses the concept of human development as an expansion of the fundamental human capability (see Chapter 2) to provide a comprehensive, albeit sad, answer to that question. More precisely, to understand why growth in market economies can deteriorate people's well-being, we will observe how the main costs of such economic growth negatively affect human development and in turn how a weakened human development can deteriorate well-being. The importance of human development in linking economic growth to well-being is due to its self-generating dynamics, which, if slowed down, increasingly weaken the resilience to rising costs of economic growth, which can thus cumulatively deteriorate people's well-being. Focusing on human development will also make it clear, in the next chapter, what conditions and actions are necessary for economic growth to ensure improvements in well-being, that is, to place human development, rather than economic growth, as a priority in individual and collective choices.

This section spells out the channels and the steps that go from market-driven economic growth, when prioritised, to the possible tendential deterioration of people's well-being. The next sections will provide some details on these channels and steps for the important domains in people's lives related to work, education, parenting, and the unfortunate case of addiction.

To follow each channel and step from economic growth to the possible decline of people's well-being, Figure 3.1 is helpful. The description will thus refer to this figure through the numbers in parentheses.

DOI: 10.4324/9781003241676-5

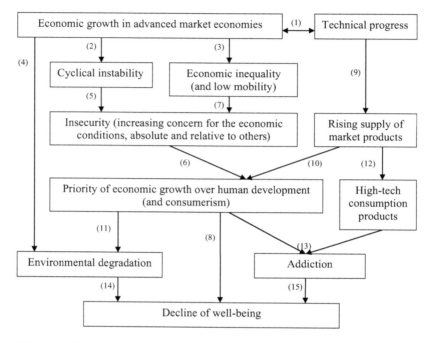

Figure 3.1 Channels and steps from economic growth to the possible decline of well-being in advanced market economies.

Economic growth in the advanced countries has been dominated by market forces, which have not only contributed to the diffusion of technical progress (1) but have also made labour markets more flexible, financial markets more dangerously powerful, and the public sector more limited. The policies have been aimed at maximising economic growth and have encouraged market forces to this aim. However, three main problems have arisen on this route: cyclical instability (2), often due to liberalised speculation on financial and other assets; economic inequality (3), mainly due to the diffusion of technical progress and the liberalisation of international markets; and environmental degradation (4), especially due to the private appropriation of natural resources as public or common goods. The first two problems are inherent in economic growth as dominated by market forces, while the environmental problem arises as an inevitable constraint to economic growth, so that this will be briefly considered later.

Cyclical instability (2), understood as alternating recessions and rapid expansions, is a source of insecurity (5) for people because it brings big changes in their lives that could be very painful, such as becoming unemployed, failing to meet basic needs, losing the usual comforts, or even having to change jobs and cities. If the trend of growth declines, cyclical instability makes unemployment and poverty the most feared eventualities. It is not necessary that people actually have such experiences to suffer from them, it is sufficient to expect them.

The fear of falling income and of failing to meet basic needs in the immediate future obviously worries people and makes them want to find economic security the most. Consequently, pursuing longer-term goals that require investment of time and other resources, such as developing people's talents and dispositions, becomes less urgent. The psychologist Abraham Maslow would say that the need for security should be satisfied before the need for self-actualisation (Maslow 1943).[1] In our words, the rise of economic insecurity induces people to focus on their individual material concern, rather than on exercising sociality-and-creativity, so they end up jeopardising the pursuit of their human development (6).

The recent global recession of 2008–2009 is the major evidence of the recurrence of cyclical instability. It has been the most severe global recession after that of the 1930s, and it has been recorded as the 12th recession after World War II in the US, while similar records hold for the other advanced countries. Since economic growth also decelerated after World War II, as shown in Chapter 1, it is not surprising that measures of people's insecurity indicate a tendency to worsen. For example, an index that captures households' losses due to falls in income not buffered by liquid financial wealth clearly indicates a steady rise of insecurity for many people since the 1970s and, at least since the mid-1980s, for virtually all income groups of the US (Hacker et al. 2014). Further evidence on the rise of insecurity and on its consequences is discussed in the next section.

The second problem inherent in the economic growth of advanced countries is *inequality* (3). Technical progress has increased the demand for skilled labour and has reduced the demand for unskilled labour, while market globalisation has compressed the wages of unskilled labour in advanced countries due to competition coming from some less advanced countries. Globalisation has also favoured financial income and the concentration of great wealth in a few hands. Moreover, economic policies have facilitated the increase of inequalities by deregulating markets and by reducing tax rates for the richest. The result can be synthesised with the following figures: having distinguished three income groups (bottom 50%, middle 40%, top 10%), the cumulative real income growth rates per adult in the US and Canada combined during the period 1980–2016 were 5%, 44%, and 123%, respectively; those in Europe were 26%, 34%, and 58%; and those of the whole world were 94%, 43%, and 70% (Chancel et al. 2018; see also Hoffman et al. 2020). In words, income growth in the US, Canada, and Europe was higher for the richest and lower for the poorest, while the opposite was true for the rest of the world as a whole.

Some evidence for the US also shows that people living in the states where income inequality is greater compare their income more strongly with that of their neighbours, thus revealing greater concern for their economic conditions (7) (Cheung & Lucas 2016). This is important evidence because it is an established fact that comparing one's income with that of others deflates subjective well-being and that the greater the importance attached to comparison, the lower the well-being.[2]

Another possible effect of the increase of inequality, concurrently with the deceleration of economic growth, is to reduce people's mobility across income groups (3).[3] This has been the case of the US since the 1940s and very probably in other advanced countries (Chetty et al. 2016; Katz & Krueger 2017).[4] But with reduced mobility, income inequality ceases over time to signal to disadvantaged people the possibility of improving their economic conditions, and this has frustrating consequences (7): some people may lose confidence in themselves, and in general, people may lose confidence in others. For example, – according to studies that merge the economic and psychology observation – greater inequality in the US has so deflated the aspirations of young people, especially those of low-income groups, that they more often choose to drop out of school (Kearney & Levine 2016; Browman et al. 2019). According to other studies, people living in the states of the US with greater economic inequality are more competitive, are less friendly towards others, and trust others less (Gould & Hijzen 2016). The European countries show similar results (Barone & Mocetti 2016).

But the combination of high aspirations to achieve ambitious life goals and the disposition to take stimulation from others' success closely reflects the twofold capability that we have called creativity-and-sociality (see Chapter 2). Therefore, we expect that greater economic inequality, together with lower income mobility, weakens human development (6), thus bringing ill-beings to people (8).

The available evidence on the case of the US from 1972 to 2008 provides a confirmation of our expectation. The increase of economic inequality of the country is significantly associated with both a decline of trust in others and a deterioration of subjective well-being of its population, with the decline of trust that significantly contributes to explain the deterioration of subjective well-being. The same role of trust is played by the perceived fairness in social relationships, which might reflect low income mobility (Oishi et al. 2011).[5] Cross-sectional evidence for 23 European countries shows that people living in countries with greater economic inequality also suffer more from subclinical depression, which is aggravated if people have reduced psychological resources, such as self-esteem, and poor relationships (van Deurzen et al. 2015). A survey of international studies on the relationship between income inequality and physical health supports the conclusion that the former causes the deterioration of the latter (Pickett & Wilkinson 2015).

The two problems of cyclical instability and economic inequality thus tend to weaken people's fundamental human development either through rising insecurity and anxiety that discourage long-term life projects or through the erosion of people's confidence in themselves and in others, that is, the erosion of the fundamental human capability inherited from the past. But the inclination of people to prioritise the goal of improving the economic conditions over human development can become effective choices if the supply of consumer products is able to satisfy such demand (9). This is indeed the case in the advanced countries, where the supply of consumer products has both offered traditional products at increasingly affordable prices and new amazing products, with the promise that all such products bring certain and immediate satisfaction.

Affordable *relative* prices increasingly come from a contrast. Whereas technical progress and, more generally, the rise of labour productivity in the economic system increase people's purchasing power, the rise of productivity in the 'production' of people's fundamental human capability is necessarily slower. Therefore, it becomes increasingly convenient spending time to work and acquire market products rather than to exercise the fundamental human capability.[6] This phenomenon is most evident by looking at the disappointing tendency in the formation of skills and competences of young and very young people in the advanced countries, as will be seen in sections 3.3 and 3.4.

Even if technical progress can accelerate human development through a range of tools to learn, find mentors, experiment with new conditions, select opportunities, and connect like-minded people, such acceleration is limited by the natural properties of changes in the human brain and body. As studies in neuroscience show, decision-making is a slow process because cognitive elaboration is relatively slow. It has to organise different areas of the brain and even of the body by drawing memory of the previous experience and combining it with perceptions. Our brains were not built for rationality but to detect news in the surrounding environment and to react for reasons of security and social bonding (Damasio 1994; Oliverio 2008). The brain is plastic in human life, but it takes time to change. Every teacher knows that learning cannot be mechanical to be effective; new notions should be connected to past experience to be useful for subsequent decisions, and this takes time (Immordino-Yang 2016). By contrast, increasing the power of the machines is reaching fantastic speeds.

Market products promise certain and immediate satisfaction through advertisement and personal experience, whereas life projects and the involvement of others to realise them are surrounded by uncertainty. Namely, human development requires selecting new opportunities that challenge individual skills, so that matching opportunities with skill inevitably leads to uncertain outcomes. People may appreciate the pursuit of human development and may find it an exciting challenge, but they should first ensure the satisfaction of basic needs and then avoid the frustration of their human capability due to falling behind others in accessing new opportunities. But these are precisely the two conditions thwarted by cyclical instability and economic inequality.

Therefore, pursuing the goal of economic growth at individual and country level and pursuing the goal of developing the fundamental human capability give rise to two different dynamics that enable us to predict which choice tends to prevail over time (6 and 10). In the first pursuit, the enjoyment of commanding over material resources makes the people essentially dependent on the dynamics of forces which drive economic growth and which are external to them. The possible consequent benefits for human development are side effects. If the time left for the development of human capability is progressively reduced, human development weakens, thus reinforcing the initial choice. In fact, the consumption of market products can become a compensation for the regret of having renounced challenges that appeared excessive. In this way, what in psychology and sociology is called 'consumerism' (and 'materialism') can find an explanation, and the emerging findings that this behaviour has detrimental effects on subjective well-being are consistent with our prediction (8).[7]

On the contrary, if the priority were human development in people's choices, thanks to the absence of adverse shocks such as poverty and social frustration, then self-sustaining dynamics would arise through the production of resources that are inner to individuals and that makes them more aware of their abilities and dispositions. As consequences, their well-being would become more resilient and their demand for market products qualitatively different. The development of creative and cooperative abilities in the population and a change in the quality of product demand could even shape a new pattern of economic growth (see Chapter 4).

In this regard, the problem of *environmental degradation* becomes relevant (4). Indeed, whereas consumerism tends to overlook the environmental problem, being rather motivated by an overwhelming personal dissatisfaction and anxiety, fundamental human development implies the respect for the environment as a form of cooperation. Therefore, to address the problem of environmental degradation due to growth in market economies, it is less effective to start with limitations on consumerism than to encourage human development because the latter implies responsible consumption and consensus for pro-environmental policies.

The contribution of industrial growth in advanced countries to environmental degradation since the past century is well known, but the direct contribution of people in their daily lives is perhaps less known. An indication comes from the evidence on food waste (11). Estimates for the US show that the waste of 900 k-calories per day per person in 1974 became 1300 in 2003, thus also reaching one quarter of the total freshwater consumption and 300 million barrels of oil per year (Hall et al. 2009).[8] Sanctions to discourage disrespectful behaviours for the environmental have a number of undesirable side-effects, according to several studies, while cooperative motivations are more effective.[9]

Environmental degradation negatively affects the well-being of the population (14). The main channel goes through the deterioration of physical health, as in the case of air pollution, but the negative effects are also direct (Orru et al. 2016).

Recent advances in technology have instead definitely strengthened the priority of consumerist choice by raising new forms of addiction, with further detrimental effects on well-being. This is a hotly debated issue, so section 3.5 will devote some space to it, but we introduce it briefly here.

Some time ago, new technologies were mostly invented to be *useful*. Machines had to relieve the fatigue of the workers, such as the cranes on construction sites, and had to help the housework, such as washing machines. The ultimate goal was to *save time* and other resources, which could then be used for other purposes. In the construction site, the saved time of the workers could be used to build other houses; at home, the saved time could be devoted to raising children. But then technology has progressively offered *pleasant* machines, or more precisely, machines and applications built to *employ people's time* and, in some cases, to employ people's peculiar skills. The first machine that had a mass impact of this sort was the television set, but since the early years of this century, there has been a great acceleration in offering products that can pleasantly engage people at any time of the day (12).

Technology is thus increasingly entering people's intimate lives. This means that people's habits change, and then their skills change.[10] Habits tend to turn into 'mild' *addiction* (13), characterised by a dramatic squeeze of time for any other activity by skills that become more specific in understanding machines rather than people. A striking example of how even working time has been squeezed is that of young men in the US. As a recent study shows, innovations to gaming and recreational computing has increased leisure time of young men and then has reduced their (market) working time by about 2.3% from 2004 to 2015, which is about 58% of the differential decline relative to older men (Aguiar et al. 2017). This is remarkable evidence for a country that has a long history of hard work as a common culture.

This addiction to the use of high-tech consumer products may be called 'mild' to distinguish it from substance addiction, which directly deteriorates health, at least in the long run. Nevertheless, this is a harmful addiction as long as it aggravates endogenously over time, it is difficult to escape, and it increasingly alters all other individual's daily behaviours and relationships with things and other people, with negative personal and social consequences. As a result, human development further weakens and could turn into a regression (13 and 15).

3.2   Adverse shocks on the labour market and on workers' well-being

The impact of technical progress on the labour market since the 1990s has been different than that of previous decades. The digitisation of machines and the automation of tasks have radically changed the demand for skills by reducing jobs with routine tasks in favour of jobs with non-routine tasks (Autor 2014; Acemoglu & Restrepo 2019). In particular, looking at the United States, whereas employment in the medium-quality jobs, as measured by hourly earnings, grew substantially in the 1960s (as is especially evident in durable manufacturing and in retail trade), it dropped in the 1990s. By contrast, employment in low-quality jobs grew substantially in the 1990s compared with the 1960s (as is especially evident in retail trade and personal services) (Wright & Dwyer 2003). As demand for most skilled workers remained high in both periods, a job polarisation in terms of education took place (Autor 2014).

These long-run trends interacted with cyclical instability. According to a study on the US economy covering the period 1967–2018, hours worked and earnings at the lower half of the male labour earnings distribution fell sharply in recessions and did not fully recover in subsequent expansions (Heathcote et al. 2020). The 2008 recession in particular further increased the polarisation of wages, although attenuating the job polarisation (Autor 2014). Another study shows that long-term unemployment remains at higher level at the end of each successive expansion since the 1950s, while short-term unemployment fluctuates along a flat trend (Krueger et al. 2014; Kroft et al. 2014). This fact reveals that technical progress makes increasing segments of the workforce permanently redundant.

The long-run negative effects of recessions on the labour market can also be observed throughout the life of workers. In fact, cohorts of workers entering the American labour market during recessions lasting at least 10 years within the period 1976–2015 report significantly lower earnings both on entry and throughout their careers (Schwandt & von Wachter 2019).[11]

But the main change in the labour market was not the tendential increase of the long-term component of unemployment, which is typical of the US, but the increase of the 'working poors' since the 1990s, which characterise all the advanced countries.[12] A detailed account of this phenomenon shows that the median real income of the 5th percentile of the distribution of lifetime income grew by 1.16% a year passing from the cohort of males that entered the labour market in 1957 (and virtually exited 31 years later) to the cohort that entered in 1967, whereas lifetime income *declined* by −0.68 between the 1967 cohort and the 1983 cohort. The polarisation of earnings is confirmed by the fact that the two percentage changes were 1.48 and −1.07 for the 25th percentile but 4.65 and 1.01 for the 99th percentile (Guvenen et al. 2017; see also Siddique 2021).

The greater risk for workers of falling into long-term unemployment, of becoming poor workers, or of being downgraded on the income scale increased their insecurity. In fact, the 10-year job retention rate declined in the private sector of the US from over 50% to less than 40%, despite the expansions of the 1980s and 1990s (Kambayashi & Kato 2017) and despite the increase of stable employment of women (Hollister & Smith 2014).[13] *Perceived* job security by workers thus declined in the US from 1977 to 2002.[14]

The effects on health are the most striking, and studies from different disciplinary perspectives tell the same dramatic story. A psychology study based on experiments shows that economic insecurity, due to both personal and contextual unemployment, and to both experienced and expected unemployment, causes physical pain and reduced pain tolerance. The psychological experience of lacking control contributes to explain these links (Chou et al. 2016). An economic study based on a very large sample including 146 nations confirms that both personal and contextual unemployment are important in explaining physical pain and adds that this especially concerns women and rich nations (Macchia & Oswald 2021).[15] These findings are surprising because conventional economic analysis would predict that in times of high unemployment, workers are less likely to incur accidents and injuries. Therefore, the physical pain seems more due to a psychological reaction to economic insecurity than actual conditions.

Indeed, economic insecurity also proves to deteriorate mental health, and not in a transitory way. A study that followed a community sample of a large US city for many years shows that the longer the involuntary unemployed status is at the age of 21–33, the more severe the self-reported mental problems, such as depression and anxiety, at the age of 39, taking into account mental health at the age of 10–12. Specifically, for each year of unemployment, the diagnosis of major depressive disorder increased by 33%, and that of anxiety disorder increased by 19% (Lee et al. 2019).[16]

The prolonged negative effects due to job insecurity are confirmed by looking at workers' well-being. The negative effects in this case are clearly demonstrated by the fact that workers who experience unemployment not only report a drop in subjective well-being beyond the pain of reduced income, but they also maintain lower levels of well-being in the case of re-employment (Lucas et al. 2004; Knabe & Raetzel 2011). The experience of unemployment – some suggest (Clark et al. 2001) – leaves a scar for the rest of life. Again, perceived job insecurity harms well-being more than actual job loss, and it persists also after the economy recovered (Geishecker 2010; Avdic et al. 2020).

Similar negative effects on well-being also seem to be caused by envy for the income of similar others, like colleagues and neighbours. It is a common finding, in fact, that living in a community with higher income reduces one's subjective well-being (Luttmer 2005; Clark et al. 2008).[17] A more specific and recent finding is that experiencing a reduction in income relative to that of others over the course of one's life from 10 to 34 years significantly reduces life satisfaction, meaning that earning £100 less than one's parents on a weekly basis reduces life satisfaction as becoming unemployed (Dolan & Lordan 2019). Moreover, the negative effects of envy on well-being and on mental health seem to persist for several years, as a very large-scale study shows (Mujcic & Oswald 2018).

But the most worrying effect of the experience of unemployment and, more generally, of economic insecurity is that of triggering unhealthy habits and addictions, so that the deterioration of workers' capabilities becomes self-aggravating. By looking at the evidence, the association between the status of unemployed and the abuse of alcohol, illicit drugs, and tobacco is strong (Compton et al. 2017), but the direction of causality is difficult to ascertain, especially if there is a vicious circle. Nevertheless, several attempts indicate that the unemployed are more likely to fall into substance abuse (Popovici & French 2013, and citations therein). One study has been also able to distinguish causation in both ways (Boden et al. 2017).

The negative effects of technical progress on the labour market do not hit only the most vulnerable workers but also the most fortunate ones. For example, a study argues and shows evidence that highly educated and high-income people in the US are particularly prone to addiction to work, called 'workaholism', with negative consequences on health, children education, and marriage (Hamermesh & Slemrod 2008).[18] According to another study, higher earnings increase time stress, holding hours of market and home work fixed, especially in the US (Hamermesh & Lee 2007). Skilled workers reported a greater drop in job satisfaction from 1995 to 2010 than unskilled workers in 15 countries of the European Union, manly due to greater work pressure (Lopes et al. 2014). A psychology study observes that excessive time pressure can frustrate creativity in jobs where workers can perform it (Baer & Olham 2006).[19]

In conclusion, the worsening of job and income conditions of workers worried them so much that they definitely concentrated their efforts on attempts to re-establish the previous economic conditions, thus giving up their possible pursuit of projects of greater self-realisation. Their subjective well-being was so reduced that they sought compensation with the secure and immediate pleasure of consuming the products they could buy, which is a well-known psychological reaction at risk of unhealthy behaviours (Sheldon & Kasser 2008; Kashdan & Breen 2007). In other words, the goal of improving the work status and the consumption possibilities has become the priority, while their fundamental human development is weakened.

This change of priority in people's choices can be also observed from the point of view of time use, which can be documented for the US. By considering the period from 1965 and 2003, time use accounting first confirms a polarisation, as graduate men reduced their weekly working hours from 49 to 45 on average, while men with high school at the most reduced their weekly working hours from 51 to 33, so that graduates in 2003 reversed their workweek relative to less educated. Graduate women increased weekly working hours from 27 to 31, while less educated women reduced weekly working hours from 18 to 15. A consequence is that graduate men reduced leisure time net of homework, which diminished thanks to market durable goods and services, and graduate women increased net leisure time. But the most interesting evidence concerns the use of net leisure time. Graduates increased the time used watching TV by 5 hours per week and reduced the time used socialising and reading books by 9 hours. Less educated people increased TV time by 9 hours per week and reduced the time used socialising and reading books by 6 hours (Aguiar & Hurst 2007).[20] Therefore, all people chose a consumption activity by sacrificing other activities that would have more favoured human development.

3.3 Education under market pressure

Education should be the main driver of human development and, in the long run, of economic growth. However, pressure from market forces has increasingly geared education towards the formation of workers for market production, while many families and sometimes governments put up only a small resistance in an attempt to keep children's education as central for life in general. Over the decades, education has thus become as pure investment to find good jobs and better social status, while education as enjoyment and development of human capability has progressively weakened.

Conventional expectation is that education is effective in driving economic growth in the long run, but by observing the advanced economies, and especially the US, this expectation is increasingly less confirmed. While the costs of education rise, its effect on economic growth diminishes. While specialised education concentrates in an elite through increasing competition, average education exhibits underwhelming performance in general competences, especially in indices that more specifically capture fundamental human capability. These facts may appear surprising, so that some room to see them in more detail is needed.

The costs of education rise for families and public finance mainly because of an economic law known as 'Baumol's cost disease' (Baumol 1967; Baumol et al. 1985). According to this law, education and other personal services such as health and cultural services display 'stagnant' or low-productivity growth with respect to the other economic sectors because employees' time in such 'stagnant' services is essential and hard to compress. Every teacher knows that the time spent to educate students is the essential core of an effective education (Dobbie & Fryer 2013; Hattie 2003; Lavy 2010), while technical devices can more help than substitute it (Bulman & Fairlie 2016; OECD 2015). By contrast, the worker in industry (or telecommunication services) knows that new machines tend to substitute her/him in an increasing number of tasks, so that each piece of production will cost less. This contrast has far-reaching implications: as technical progress becomes more effective in industrial production, purchasing products becomes more convenient than financing educational services, or, in reverse terms, a unit of education becomes more costly than a unit of industrial production. A consequence is that teachers' pay tends to be reduced in order to limit costs, with detrimental effects on the quality of education.

An accurate study by William Baumol and colleagues confirms that total costs of education, measured in proportion of gross domestic product, increased substantially from 1998 to 2007 in the US and other advanced countries. This result applies to primary, secondary, and tertiary education, and it takes into account the increasing number of students relative to the population. In particular, teachers' costs, which are the most substantial ones, grow more than the other costs (Wolff et al. 2014). Other studies show evidence, though less detailed, consistent with 'Baumol's cost disease' in the US educational sector for the whole post–World War II period (Archibald & Feldman 2008; Dragomirescu-Gaina 2015).

To increase the productivity in the education system, this has been made more similar to the market production system. This is evident from the definition of common standards that students and schools should achieve

(Bishop 2010), from the ranking of schools and universities according to common measures and from the use of vouchers to finance education so that parents can choose the schools for their children like any other market product. All of this contributes to improving the signal that education, as human productive capital, shows to producers.

The most innovative firms, in particular, can easily concentrate their labour demand on the most educated workforce. Admission to college thus becomes a requirement for aspiring to a good job, with the consequence of fuelling a fierce competition for such admission with a further increase of educational costs. In fact, the percentage of senior students who applied to top public colleges in the US grew from 7.5 in 1972 to 12.8 in 2004, and in the case of top private colleges the percentage grew from 3.9 to 6.2, while accepted students dropped by about 24% in both cases. The costs of education further increased because of students' extra preparation for college admission (Ramey & Ramey 2010; Bound et al. 2009).

To make the finances of families and governments sustainable, increasing costs of education would require increasing returns to education. However, returns to education do not seem to be growing enough but rather seem to have decelerated sharply after the 1990s (Oreopoulos & Petronijevic 2014:Fig. 3), while the voucher system does not work as expected, at least in the US (Macleod & Uequiola 2019). One reason for this failure is that parents' school choices for their children seem to be unrelated to school effectiveness but rather follow peers' quality (Abdulkadiroglu et al. 2020). Another reason can be found in evidence that compares disadvantaged students who obtained the voucher via random lottery with students who did not obtain it but equally disadvantaged. The result is that the former scored lower in math, reading, science, and social studies (Abdulkadiroglu et al. 2018). Other reasons for pessimism are that growth in advanced economies is decelerating, as noted in Chapter 1, and that education spending in families' and governments' budgets is beginning to show severe signs of stress.[21]

Attempts to limit the costs of education are thus inevitable. A study focusing on the US shows that productivity growth in manufacturing from 1997 to 2010 was accompanied by a *reduction* of the number of teachers per 1000 pupils (Chen & Moul 2014). Another way to limit teacher costs is to relatively reduce the growth of their salary. This actually took place in the US, since the proportion of non-teaching employees with a lower salary than teachers diminished from 1940 to 2010, especially in the case of young teachers (Hanushek 2016).

But lower compensation for teachers than for other employees likely means lower quality of education and hence of students' motivations and competences. A study based on a cross-section of advanced countries in fact concludes that recruiting less able individuals in teaching and hindering fast salary advancement as in other jobs have a negative effect on pupil results (Dolton & Marcenaro-Gutierrez 2011).[22] The reduction of students' competences can be documented for the US according to a number of dimensions: a reduction of reading competence among 17-year-old students from early 1990s to 2008 (Reardon et al. 2012), a reduction in academic achievement in high school from 1992 to 2012 (Judson & Hobson 2015; Bound et al. 2009), a reduction in the completion rate of tertiary education in 22-year-old students from the 1970s to early 2000 (Bound et al. 2007), and a reduction in the automaticity in word recognition by both children and adolescents in 2001 compared to their 1960s counterparts (Spichtig et al. 2016).

More direct indicators of the fundamental human capability of American students also show a worsening performance, according to the available evidence. For example, trust in others among late adolescents has declined from 1976 to 2012 (Twenge et al. 2014). Regarding work values, the 18-year-old generation of students in 2006 attached less importance to interest and engagement and to make friends on the workplace compared with same-age generation of students in 1976 (while attaching greater importance to leisure, pay, and status) (Twenge et al. 2010). Regarding life values, the first-year generation of college students in 2009 attached less importance to having a meaningful life than the generation of the same age in 1976 (while attaching greater importance to being rich) (Twenge et al. 2012). Empathy (i.e., feeling worried about less fortunate people) and "the ability to imagine how things look from others' perspective" declined from 1979 to 2009 among college students, independent from the differences in their economic conditions (Konrath et al. 2011). The feeling of being in control of life events also declined both in schoolchildren aged 9 to 14 from the 1970s to the 1990s and in college students from the 1960s to the 1990s (Twenge et al. 2004). Finally, creative thinking, measured as elaboration of new ideas, declined in both kindergarten and school children from 1984 to 2017 (Kim 2011, 2021).

Therefore, having started from the economic law of 'cost disease' applied to education, we conclude that a lot of evidence on the US case often drawn from psychology studies, and based on rather large samples, sometimes representative of the country and sometimes organised as meta-analysis, points in the same worrying long-run direction where students' human development is weakening.

3.4   Parenting and children's development under market pressure

Technical progress and economic growth have undoubtedly achieved great successes in children's development, such as the drop in mortality rates, in infectious diseases, in malformations. More doubtful is whether the growing market pressure on children, and hence on parenting, has helped to improve their well-being, especially in the advanced countries. In fact, doubts arise when the focus shifts from children's physical health to the development of their mental capability.

Economics has contributed to understanding children's development, especially thanks to the Nobel laureate James Heckman, who has given impetus to an interdisciplinary stream of studies on this matter. One of his main contributions is to define the optimal development of children's cognitive and socio-emotional skills for given external resources, such as parents' educational time and family's economic conditions. The usual failure observed in achieving such optimum thus raises the question about the reason for such failure, and about the role of markets in this unfortunate outcome.

Optimal development of children's skills – according to Heckman and colleagues – should take into account a number of its natural properties. First, "skills beget skills", and, in particular, socio-emotional skills affect cognitive skills and can help them even beyond the young age. This is fully consistent with the property that human development is self-sustaining (see Chapter 2).[23] Second, the development of children's skills depends more on parents' educational time and skill than on familiar economic conditions, at least when considering the case of the US (Kautz et al. 2014).[24] This can also be observed in behavioural, academic, and labour outcomes in later ages. Third, the effects of parents' investments are greater the better the investments at an earlier age are, so that the estimated rate of return on investment in 3-year-olds can reach as much as 10% per annum (Heckman 2008).

The importance of parents' educational time in early education has been documented in several instances. A study based on a large sample of British children shows that the more mothers spend time with their 3-year-old children by engaging in educational activities such as teaching, playing together, and reading, the greater the verbal and socio-emotional skills of the child 4 years later (Del Bono et al. 2014). Studies in neuroscience confirm the special importance of time devoted to children in their first years of life (Neidell 2000; Rao et al. 2010).

No less important in early education is parents' educational skill. A well-known perspective for qualifying parenting skills distinguishes the 'authoritative' parenting style, which is the best, from the 'authoritarian' and 'permissive' styles. In the first, the parents propose themselves to the child as reliable references, as they both respect and monitor her/him; in the second, instead the parents impose their will on the child without too much argument; in the third, the parents make the child little responsible, as they always remain at her/his service (Baumrind 1967).

As suggested by the psychologists of education Lev S. Vygotsky and Jean Piaget, parents' and teachers' educational skill essentially consists in understanding the child's skill level by observing her/his realisations and in responding with adequate challenging tasks for her/him, meaning adequate complexity and adequate activities, possibly in collaboration with other children. Early education should thus develop both social and creative skill because 'learning' does not simply mean absorbing new information; rather, it is the creation of new structures based on pre-existing personal knowledge (Vygotsky 1978[1930]; Piaget 1973; Heckman et al. 2013). Therefore, children can better develop skills in certain tasks than in others and, when adults, can better specialise in some activities. This is again fully consistent with our formulation of human development.

Technical progress and economic growth provide a lot of means and opportunities that could be used to maximise children's education. However, the market forces involved are pushing in a different direction.

Parents are subject to the Baumol's law of 'costs disease' (see section 3.1 and 3.3), when deciding how to use their time on daily, weekly, or longer time basis. In fact, since educational time is hard to compress without deteriorating children's education, using time in educational activities appears to parents more costly and with more uncertain effects than working and furnishing their children with more market products, which new technologies produce in ever greater quantity and quality. This tendency discourages investing time in children's education.

The cultural change of women's emancipation has contributed to increasing their participation in the labour market and to make them more independent, but it has also contributed to increase their education and, consequently, to better appreciate the value of educating children. The tendency to reduce educational time for children can thus be contrasted with the tendency to improve parents' educational skill.

To evaluate this contrast, let us begin to look at the first tendency. The increase of women's participation in the labour market in recent decades, especially in the advanced countries, is well known, but the consequences on children are less known. As several studies show, working mothers, on average, devote less time to their children than non-working mothers, and the greater time devoted by fathers is not compensating (Hsin & Felfe 2014).[25] To aggravate this phenomenon, the status of single mothers has become a more frequent case.[26] According to a study on a representative sample of young American mothers, the effects on children's cognitive skills are negative if the mother works during children's first year of life, even if childcare services are used. These negative effects become substantial if the mother works more than 20 hours a week and seem to persist until children's school age (James-Burdumy 2005).[27] Even children in better socio-economic conditions suffer from negative effects on the cognitive and socio-emotional skills because of working mothers (Ruhm 2018).

Fortunately, the proportion of educated mothers is increasing over time, and a welcome established fact is that educated mothers devote more time to their children than less educated mothers (Hsin & Felfe 2014; Guryan et al. 2008). However, it is not clear what the net effect on children's education is due to parents' tendencies to work more (and hence to leave their children more alone) and to devote more skilled time to them because the parents themselves are better educated.

To solve this ambiguity, let us take a closer look at parents' investments in their children and how parents' educational skill is effective under the market pressures. Parents' own education seems indeed to be important for performing effective educational activities for their children, especially for developing cognitive skills. However, the authoritative parenting style, which is generally not part of parents' formal education, seems to count much more for children's development of socio-emotional skills, such as the internal locus of control (Fiorini & Keane 2014; Cobb-Clark et al. 2019).[28] Moreover, there is some evidence for the US that the recent increase in the time devoted to children, especially by educated parents, is concentrated on children's adolescence rather than on their infancy, thus going in the opposite direction to what Heckman prescribed to reach the optimal time profile of educational investments. One reason for this seems the increasing need to prepare children for college admission, thus confirming the priority for higher income (Ramey & Ramey 2010).

The crux is that parenting skills are just an unnecessary side effect of parents' own education, which was rather aimed at finding a good job. Such parenting skill must be confronted with the growing pressure of producers to sell products for children. On the one side, parents' goal could be, at best, to maximise children's healthy development, taking market products for children as a means. On the other side, producers' goal is to maximise their sales, taking the educational aspects of their products as a mere market opportunity. Parents are not professional in educating their children, whereas producers are professional in selling their products because they are so disciplined by the market (Pugno 2009). Parents act individually or in small groups, whereas producers act with advertisements across the country, thus more likely forming social fads, which adds peer pressure to producers' pressure on single parents.

Furthermore, parents need to learn how to manage new products for children to make them useful educational aids. However, such products are designed to be immediately attractive, while educational content is subordinate, unnecessary, or even perverse if observed from the human development perspective. In fact, many products for children point to develop competition with others, real or virtual, rather than cooperation. The typical example is violent video games that have become popular among young people. While it has been questioned whether playing such games causes an increase in overt aggression (Della Vigna & La Ferrara 2015), a number of studies in the laboratory demonstrates the effect of desensitisation to represented violence over time through less empathy for victims (Brockmyer 2015; Greitemeyer & McLatchie 2011; Haslam 2006). The rise of the representation of violence in the media has been ascertained, at least, for the rate of gun violence in popular American TV dramas from 2000 to 2018 (Jamieson & Romer 2021).[29]

The attraction for the violent video games is prepared for younger children by another popular play product, namely Lego. This consists of a variety of 'bricks' for building complex games and representations. According to a recent calculation, the various types of bricks representing weapons have increased in proportion to the total types from almost zero in the early 1980s to 30% in 2015 (Bartneck et al. 2016).

Therefore, the confrontation between parents and producers in influencing children's development has become increasingly unequal. Obviously, parents can mediate between the use of video games, television, and the Internet and the effects on their children, for example, by imposing restrictions. But a large-scale study suggests that such mediation changes very little children's behaviour (Collier et al. 2016).

To conclude, there are various reasons for predicting that market forces operate more *against* than *for* the development of children's mental capability. This is a paradox for an economist who is very confident in the power of markets to optimally solve the problem of coordinating the pursuits of individuals' goals. Where, then, is the market failure?

In the child–parent relationship, parents offer an 'educational service' in exchange of children's future goods and services when they are old (Becker et al. 2016). However, whereas parents can choose to invest resources in children (and insure against bad outcomes), children cannot choose parents' 'educational service' because there is no market for it. If children could choose the 'educational service' in a free market, parents offering the worst 'educational service' would exit the market, and children would learn to optimise their development. Instead, bad parenting survives by not being sanctioned by the market as this does not exist.

3.5   Addiction as self-medication

Addiction can be considered a disease because it alters the functioning of the body and of the brain in particular and because there is a genetic predisposition that differs among persons. However, much empirical evidence shows that addiction is also the consequence of adverse conditions and of unfortunate choices.[30] For example, disadvantaged social and economic conditions in early childhood – according to Heckman et al. (2006, 2013) – weaken the development of cognitive and socio-emotional skills, and this causes an increase in the likelihood of smoking and using marijuana in young adulthood. Other studies in economics and epidemiology specify that risk factors for substance or gambling addiction are the loss of the father; having a working mother; child abuse; or, in adulthood, prolonged unemployment and more generally stressful thoughts and boredom (Pudney 2004; Lane et al. 2016; Bergevin et al. 2006; LePera 2011). Studies in psychology of 'attachment', which is a reassuring bond with the caregiver in childhood and with an intimate figure in adulthood, show that adults with 'insecure' attachments engage in risky behaviours more frequently in an attempt to avoid negative thoughts. In particular, adults with 'avoidant' attachment try not to think about having avoided social relationships, and in the case of 'anxious' attachment, people try to avoid ruminating over painful past events (Mikulincer & Shaver 2007).[31]

The role of choice in triggering addiction can be strengthened by the contingent appeal of addictive substances and behaviours, which promise pleasure and euphoria or simply distraction from painful thoughts. The appeal is stronger if the addictive substances and behaviours are cheap and easily available.

The choice component of addiction is evident because many people regret having undertaken risky behaviours, and many others pay psychological services to overcome addiction. For example, although intensive television watching may be considered one of the least harmful addictions, there is no doubt that this behaviour often leaves people regretful, thus reducing their life satisfaction. One reason seems to be that television watching relentlessly stimulates the aspirations for consumption and status (Frey et al. 2007; Benesch et al. 2010; Bruni & Stanca 2008; Hyll & Schneider 2013). Another example of regret is that of smokers who, having failed to quit smoking, were happy with the various restrictions in public spaces that have been imposed in recent years (Odermatt & Stutzer 2015).

The choice component in undertaking risky behaviours is further observed in laboratory experiments[32] and even in the tragic 'natural' experiment of the American soldiers in the Vietnam War, whose frequent substance addiction dwindled to a minority of them once they returned home.[33]

It is important to underline the component of choice because this allows us to focus on the individual conditions of ill-being that prevailed *before* falling into the addiction, which *then* can become a trap. This shift of the focus has a number of advantages. First, addiction can be viewed as an attempt to self-medicate, thus opening the way to link weak fundamental human development to addiction. Second, the typical characteristics of addiction, that is, self-harm, withdrawal symptoms, tolerance, and alteration of ordinary behaviours, become less crucial, so that the range of potential addictive products and behaviours can be extended. For example, the mentioned television watching is little self-harming, although it takes time, which could be alternatively used in more constructive and satisfactory way (Bruni & Stanca 2008).[34] Third, the inclusion of such 'mild' addictions makes risky behaviours much more popular and manageable and even masked by ordinary forms of consumption. Fourth, the attempt to self-medicate from the underlying ill-being may induce individuals both to under-estimate the harmful long-term consequences of addictions, which may be perfectly known, and to over-estimate the expected pleasure derived from risky behaviours.[35]

The problem of addiction in advanced countries is undoubtedly on the rise. Some heavy addictions have greatly increased in recent times, although the long-run trend of smoking has diminished. High-tech addictions, as (possibly) mild addictions, have spread widely.

As the most striking fact, US President Donald Trump declared on 27 October 2017 the opioid crisis as a national health emergency. Opioids, which are natural psychoactive substances such as opium derivatives, or synthetic substances such as fentanyl, have in fact spread illegally in the US at an astonishing rate. Opioid overdose deaths increased 3.6 times from 1999 to 2017. Nor can all of this be easily blamed on the 2008 economic crisis (CDC 2018; Ruhm 2018; Blanchflower & Graham 2020). Although the prevalence of opioids in the US is a multiple of that in the rest of the world, some trends are also worrying in Europe. In England and Wales, male deaths from the use of new and old psychoactive substances tripled from 1993 to 2015 (EMCDDA 2017; ONS 2017). In Italy, the index of frequent intakes of psychoactive substances in the student population is on the rise since 2005–2006 (ESPAD 2015; Governo italiano 2017).

The mild addiction that spread the most in the last 15 years is that of high-tech products, an absolute novelty in terms of impact and size. According to various studies in psychology and neuroscience, the prolonged use of smartphones, tablets, and personal computers can give rise to an addiction similar in some respects to the more well-known substance addictions. In fact, it is observed that when, for example, video games are used, the production of dopamine in human brains, also called the pleasure neurotransmitter, is stimulated in a similar way to when taking drugs. Similarly, when the intensive use of video games is stopped, dopamine production is inhibited, thus causing the unpleasant sensation of abstinence (Kross et al. 2013; Allcott et al. 2020). In confirmation of this, it was found, through some laboratory exercises, that intensive use of social media reduces people's satisfaction with their lives, and its interruption increases it, and that such use forms a habit (Allcott et al. 2020; Tromholt 2016; Pénard & Mayol 2017).

The high-tech addiction does not seem to be due to a genetic predisposition but rather to the environmental context, which unfortunately has two additional pitfalls compared with substance addiction. The first emerges from the use of the same technological products in normal family and working life. It is therefore difficult to cease the consumption of these products for those who want to 'detoxify'. The second pitfall is due to updating and continuous innovations, which are conceived and designed so that these products are used as much as possible by anyone, adults, adolescents, and children (Montag & Reuter 2015; Alter 2018).

The intensive use of high-tech products can cause a harmful addiction, which is signalled by various symptoms of malaise, such as greater difficulty in paying prolonged attention, remembering past events, making complex reasoning, relating to others, and trusting others, thus causing a tendency towards isolation and to entertain mainly virtual relationships (Turkle 2011; Kross et al. 2013; Sabatini & Sarracino 2017). It was also calculated how much high-tech consumption must be prolonged to deteriorate people's well-being. From this calculation, based on a sample of over 120,000 people, it seems that in the cases of video games and smartphones, just 2 hours are enough to observe that the positive effects become negative and worsen as the use is prolonged throughout the day. In the case of videos and personal computers for recreational use, the turning point seems to be around 4 hours (Przybylski & Weinstein 2017).

Disturbing correlations have even been found between use of high-tech products and suicidal thoughts as well as depressive symptoms. Based on a representative sample of the US youth population, a study shows that teens who use these products for 3 hours a day or more are 34% more likely to have suicidal thoughts than teens who use them less than 2 hours, regardless of their social background. Teenagers who use social media every day are significantly more likely to have depressive symptoms than others, provided they do not also have real, not just virtual social relationships, and, surprisingly, they are female (Twenge et al. 2018). In fact, only the depressive symptoms of female adolescents have been increasing since 2010. According to another study, the increase in free time that occurred among young males from 2004 to 2015 in the US was almost entirely dedicated to recreational activities on personal computers, mainly on video games (Aguiar et al. 2017).

To conclude, identifying and weighting the various contextual conditions that induce people to choose behaviours at risk of addiction, both substance and 'mild' addiction, is undoubtedly difficult. However, some conclusions can be drawn. First, adverse economic shocks do matter but are neither sufficient not necessary causes. For example, the dramatic changes in the labour market in the recent decades have likely fuelled the American opioid crisis (Charles et al. 2018), but other causes have also been surely at work (Maclean et al. 2020). Second, adverse parenting conditions during infancy and adolescence can be the crucial cause in the most severe cases. More frequently, such initial conditions form pre-dispositions that may significantly contribute together with other factors to undertake risky behaviours in adulthood (Powdthavee 2014). Third, the drop in subjective well-being is a useful signal to predict the risk of falling into addictive behaviours (Moschion & Powdthavee 2017). Finally, high-tech devices that we use daily (and see others intensively use) are terribly useful but also terribly dangerous because they may become an addiction without being recognised as such.

Notes

1   The fact that human needs have priorities consistent with Maslow's prediction has been shown for a sample of 123 countries (Tay & Diener 2011).
2   See Luttmer (2005) and Alderson et al. (2012) for the US and Clark & Senik (2010) for Europe.
3   Increasing inequality also tends to worsen cyclical instability, as well as the other way around, as Stiglitz (2012) explains.
4   Insufficient data for countries other than the US unfortunately prevent firm conclusions (Stuhler 2018).
5   Evidence for a panel of 28 European countries from 1992 to 2019 shows consistent results by rather considering 'perceived' inequality (Hajdu 2021). Bartolini et al. (2013) show that the decline of subjective well-being in the US is mainly due to comparing one's income with that of others and to the decline of trust.
6   This is an application of the so-called Baumol's law of the 'rising cost disease', originally referred to labour-intensive service production (Baumol 1967).
7   DeSarbo & Edwards (1996) identify motivations for 'compulsive buying' in insecurity and anxiety and, more specifically, in the lack of self-esteem and of the ability to control life events. See Sheldon & Kasser (2008) on the link between insecurity and extrinsic motivations and Dittmar et al. (2014) on the link between materialism and ill-being.
8   For estimates of food waste in Europe, see Bräutigam et al. (2014).
9   See Pugno & Sarracino (2021) and the studies cited therein.
10   For an economic formalisation of habit formation, though in rational way, see Becker & Murphy (1988). A similar process, but not rational, is described by Stiglitz (2008).
11   See Oreopoulos et al. (2012) and Cutler et al. (2015) for similar results in other advanced countries.
12   Other problematic changes in the labour market due to technical progress and, as partial consequence, to markets globalisation are the decline in the income labour share and the increase of mismatches between education and jobs and between competences and tasks (see D'Orlando & Ferrante 2021).
13   In Germany, where employment protection is stronger, layoffs rather than voluntary quits also increased in the years before the 2008 crisis (Bergemann & Mertens 2011). The case of the UK is similar (Green 2009).

14 This decline is estimated even after controlling for unemployment (Fullerton & Wallace 2007). West Germany (Bergemann & Mertens 2011), France (Givord & Maurin 2004), and the UK (Green 2009) report similar changes.

15 According to a study focused on Germany, young adults who enter the labour market in a recession suffer from worse health and even exhibit greater probability of death in middle age (Schwandt & von Wachter 2020).

16 A study based on panel data available for Germany shows that both employed and unemployed workers who report job insecurity also report low scores of mental health averaging 2.5 years (Otterbach & Souza-Poza 2016). See also Caroli & Godard (2016), who use a sample of 22 European countries; Colantone et al. (2015), who show a negative effect of import competition and thus the underlying job insecurity on workers' mental distress in the UK; and Kopasker et al. (2018), who focus on anticipating insecure employment and the effects on mental health in the UK.

17 According to Hounkpatin et al. (2015), income rank is a better predictor of subsequent depressive symptoms than own income.

18 Keynes (1930) already predicted such form of addiction.

19 The economic study Gross (2018) finds that excessive competition reduces creativity.

20 Sevilla et al. (2012) confirm these results.

21 The share of undergraduate students taking out loans increased from 19% to 35% in the 1989–2008 period, so that the total volume of federal student loans expanded sevenfold, and less than half of graduating students had more than $100,000 of student debt (Oreopoulos & Petronijevic 2014).

22 Similar results are in Hanushek et al. (2014), which found a close positive correlation between teachers' competences and their students' competences in higher schools, having considered math and literacy competences.

23 Emotional skill in childhood is the strongest predictor of life satisfaction in adulthood, according to Layard et al. (2014) and Flèche et al. (2021).

24 See also Del Boca et al. (2014), who show, on the basis of a sample of 3500 children in the US, http://www.econ.ucla.edu/workingpapers/wp806.pdf that parental time improves child quality when s/he is young more than money expenditures for her/him. This is also confirmed by Loken et al. (2012) for the case of Norway.

25 A causal analysis shows that work induces women to reduce the time devoted to children's educational activities (Cawley & Liu 2007).

26 For example, in the US, children aged less than 5 years with both working parents were about one third in 1967, whereas they were two thirds in 2009 (Fox et al. 2013). This tendency is only slightly attenuated in other advanced countries (Sayer & Gornick 2012).

27 See also Bernal (2008), Aizer (2004). Similar results have been obtained for the UK (Ermisch & Francesconi 2013).

28 Lekfuangfu et al. (2016) show the importance of mothers' internal locus of control for predicting time investments in her child and the child's cognitive skills.

29 This study further shows that the rising trend of gun violence on TV is significantly correlated with homicides attributable to firearms.

30 For the controversy on whether substance addiction is a disease or is a matter of choice, see Ross (2010).

31 Stressful events can moderate the relationship between the attachment style and gaming addiction (Sung et al. 2020).

32 For example, a group of people was proposed in an experiment to gamble after asking them to list the negative aspects of their character, thus inducing unpleasant thoughts. It emerged that this group, compared with the control group that had not previously been induced any unpleasant thoughts, played with higher stakes, more frequently, and with faster decisions (Rockloff et al. 2011).

33 The sample of the American soldiers who went to Vietnam was quite random due to the then military conscription. The jump from the US to Vietnam was shocking for them, and heroin and cocaine were easily available for them in those new conditions, so most soldiers became addicted. Once they returned home, however, only a minority resumed taking drugs, and of this minority, most came from problematic families or used drugs even before leaving for the war. This minority had conditions of origin similar to those of the other drug users who remained at home (Robins & Slobodyan 2003).

34 A crowding-out effect clearly emerges in a laboratory experiment from using Facebook to spending time with friends and family (Allcott et al. 2020).

35 A fifth advantage is that the policy implication of giving priority to population's human development is more effective than restricting the focus on alleviating addictions.

References

Abdulkadiroglu A, Pathak P, Walters C (2018) Free to choose. *American Economic Journal: Applied Economics* 10:175–206

Abdulkadiroglu A, Pathak PA, Schellenberg J, Christopher R (2020) Do parents value school effectiveness? *NBER Working Paper*, No. 23912. Cambridge, MA, https://www.nber.org/papers/w23912

Acemoglu D, Restrepo P (2019) Automation and new tasks. *Journal of Economic Perspectives* 33(2):3–30

Aguiar M, Bils M, Charles KK, Hurst E (2017) Leisure luxuries and the labor supply of young men. *NBER Working Paper*, No. 23552. Cambridge, MA, https://www.nber.org/papers/w23552

Aguiar, M, Hurst E (2007) Measuring trends in leisure. *Quarterly Journal of Economics* 122(3):969–1006

Aizer A (2004) Home alone: Supervision after school and child behavior. *Journal of Public Economics* 88:1835–1848

Alderson AS, Katz-Gerro T (2012) Compared to whom? *Social Forces* 95(1):25–53

Allcott H, Braghieri L, Eichmeyer S (2020) The welfare effects of social media. *American Economic Review* 110(3):629–676

Alter A (2018) *Irresistible: The Rise of Addictive Technology and the Business of Keeping us Hooked.* Penguin, London

Archibald RB, Feldman DH (2008) Explaining increases in higher educational costs. *Journal of Higher Education* 79(3):268–295

Autor D (2014) Polanyi' paradox and the shape of employment growth. *NBER Working Paper*, No. 20485. Cambridge, MA, https://www.nber.org/papers/w20485

Avdic D, de New SC, Kamhöfer DA (2020) Economic downturns and mental wellbeing. *DICE Discussion Paper*, No. 337, Duesseldorf, https://www.econstor.eu/bitstream/10419/216731/1/1696937833.pdf

Baer M, Olham GR (2006) The curvilinear relation between experienced creative time pressure and creativity. *Journal of Applied Psychology* 91(4):963–970

Barone G, Mocetti S (2016) Inequality and trust. *Economic Inquiry* 54(2):794–809

Bartneck C, Min Ser Q, Moltchanova E, Smithies J (2016) Have LEGO products become more violent? *PLoS ONE* 11(5):e0155401

Bartolini S, Bilancini E, Pugno M (2013) Did the decline in social connections depress Americans' happiness. *Social Indicators Research* 110(3):1033–1059

Baumol WJ (1967) Macroeconomics of unbalanced growth. *American Economic Review* 57:415–426

Baumol WJ, Batey Blackman SA, Wolff N (1985) Unbalanced growth revisited. *American Economic Review* 75(4):806–817

Baumrind D (1967) Child care practices anteceding three patterns of preschool. *Genetic Psychology Monographs* 75(1):43–88

Becker GS, Murphy KM (1988) A theory of rational addiction. *Journal of Political Economy* 96(4):675–700

Becker GS, Murphy KM, Spenkuch JL (2016) The manipulation of children's preferences, old age support, and investment in children's human capital. *Journal of Labor Economics* 34:S3–S30

Benesch C, Frey BS, Stutzer A (2010) TV channels, self control and happiness. *B.E. Journal of Economic Analysis & Policy* 10(1), Article 86

Bergemann A, Mertens A (2011) Job stability trends, lay-offs, and transitions to unemployment in West Germany. *Labour* 25(4):421–446

Bergevin T, Gupta R, Derevensky J, Kaufman F (2006) Adolescent gambling. *Journal of Gambling Studies* 22:195–208

Bernal R (2008) The effect of maternal employment and child care on children cognitive development. *International Economic Review* 49(4):1173–1209

[Bishop] JH (2010) Which secondary education systems work best? Cornell University. *ILR Working Paper*, No. 105 Retrieved [23 Feb. 2022] from Cornell University, ILR School site: https://ecommons.cornell.edu/handle/1813/74587

Blanchflower DG, Graham C (2020) Happiness and aging in the United States. *NBER Working Paper*, No. 28143. Cambridge, MA, https://www.nber.org/papers/w28143

Boden JM, Lee JO, Grest CV, McLeod GFH (2017) Modelling possible causality in the associations between unemployment, cannabis use, and alcohol misuse. *Social Science & Medicine* 175:127–134

Bound J, Brad H, Bridget TL (2009) Playing the admissions game. *Journal of Economic Perspectives* 23(4):119–146

Bound J, Lovenheim M, Turner SE (2007) Understanding the decrease in college completion rates and the increased time to the Baccalaureate degree. *Population Studies Center Research Report 2007 07–626*. University of Michigan, https://www.psc.isr.umich.edu/pubs/rr07-626171f.pdf?i=925974015614108924178076177&f=rr07-626.pdf

Bräutigam K-R, Joerissen J, Priefer C (2014) The extent of food waste generation across EU-27. *Waste Management & Research* 32(8):683–94

Brockmyer JF (2015) Playing violent video games and desensitization to violence. *Child and Adolescent Psychiatric Clinics of North America* 24:65–77

Browman AS, Destin M, Kearney MS, et al. (2019) How economic inequality shapes mobility expectations and behaviour in disadvantaged youth. *Nature Human Behavior* 3:214–220

Bruni L, Stanca L (2008) Watching alone. *Journal of Economic Behavior & Organization* 65(3–4):506–528

Bulman G, Fairlie RW (2016) Technology and education. *NBER Working Paper*, No. 22237. Cambridge, MA, https://www.nber.org/papers/w22237

Caroli E, Godard, M (2016) Does job insecurity deteriorate health? *Health Economics* 25(2):131–147

Cawley J, Liu F (2007) Mechanisms for the association between maternal employment and child cognitive development. *NBER Working Paper*, No. 13609. Cambridge, MA, https://www.nber.org/papers/w13609

CDC – Centers for Disease Control and Prevention (2018) Drug overdose deaths in the United States, 1999–2017. *NCHS Data Bief*, No. 329 – November 2018, https://www.cdc.gov/nchs/data/databriefs/db329-h.pdf

Chancel L, Alvaredo F, Piketty T, et al. (2018) *World Inequality Report*. World Inequality Lab, https://wir2018.wid.world/files/download/wir2018-full-report-english.pdf

Charles KK, Hurst E, Schwartz M (2018) The transformation of manufacturing and the decline in U.S. employment. *NBER Working Paper*, No. 24468. Cambridge, MA, https://www.nber.org/papers/w24468

Chen X, Moul CC (2014) Disease or utopia? *Economics Letters* 122:220–223

Chetty R, Grusky D, Hell M, Hendren N, Manduca R, Narang J (2016) The fading American dream. *NBER Working Paper*, No. 22910. Cambridge, MA, https://www.nber.org/papers/w22910

Cheung F, Lucas RE (2016) Income inequality is associated with stronger social comparison effects. *Journal of Personality in Social Psychology* 110(2):332–341

Chou EY, Parmar BL, Galinsky AD (2016) Economic insecurity increases physical pain. *Psychological Science* 27(4):443–454

Clark AE, Frijters P, Shields M (2008) Relative income, happiness and utility. *Journal of Economic Literature* 46(1):95–144

Clark AE, Georgellis Y, Sanfey P (2001) Scarring. *Economica* 68:221–241

Clark AE, Senik C (2010) Who compares to whom? *Economic Journal* 120:573–594

Cobb-Clark DA, Salamanca N, Zhu A (2019) Parenting style as an investment in human development. *Journal of Population Economics* 32:1315–1352

Colantone I, Crinò R, Ogliari L (2015) The hidden cost of globalization. *CESifo Working Paper*, No. 5586, https://papers.ssrn.com/sol3/papers.cfm?abstract_id=2694447

Collier KM, Coyne SM, Hawkins AJ, et al. (2016) Does parental mediation of media influence child outcomes? *Developmental Psychology* 52(5):798–812

Compton WM, Conway KP, Stinson FS, Grant BF (2017) Changes in the prevalence of major depression and comorbid substance use disorders in the United States between 1991–1992 and 2001–2002. *American Journal of Psychiatry* 163:2141–2147

Cutler DM, Huang W, Lleras-Muney A (2015) When does education matter? *Social Science & Medicine* 127:63–73

D'Orlando F, Ferrante F, Oliveiro A (2021) *Economic Change and Wellbeing*. Routledge, Abingdon

Damasio AR (1994) *Descartes' Error*. Avon Books, New York

Del Boca D, Flinn C, Wiswall M (2014) Household choices and child development. *Review of Economic Studies* 81:137–185

Del Bono E, Francesconi M, Kelly Y, Sacker A (2016) Early maternal time investment and early child outcomes. *Economic Journal* 126(596):F96–F135

Della Vigna S, La Ferrara E (2015) Economic and social impacts of the media. In S Anderson, J Waldfogel, D Stromberg (eds) *Handbook of Media Economics*. Vol. 1A. Elsevier, Amsterdam, Ch. 19

DeSarbo WS, Edwards EA (1996) Typologies of compulsive buying behavior. *Journal of Consumer Psychology* 5(3):231–262

Dittmar H, Bond R, Hurst M, Kasser T (2014) The relationship between materialism and personal well-being: A meta-analysis. *Personality Processes and Individual Differences* 107(5):879–924

Dobbie W, Fryer R (2013) Getting beneath the veil of effective schools. *American Economic Journal: Applied Economics* 5(4):28–60

Dolan P, Lordan G (2019) Climbing up ladders and sliding down snakes. *IZA DP*, No. 12519, https://docs.iza.org/dp12519.pdf

Dolton P, Marcenaro-Gutierrez OD, Pistaferri L, Algan Y (2011) If you pay peanuts do you get monkeys? *Economic Policy* 26(65):5–55

Dragomirescu-Gaina C (2015) An empirical inquiry into the determinants of public education spending in Europe. *IZA Journal Labor Studies* 4:25

EMCDDA – European Monitoring Centre for Drugs and Drug Addiction (2017) *European Drug Report 2017: Trends and Developments*. Luxembourg: Publications Office of the European Union

Ermisch J, Francesconi M (2013) The effect of parental employment on child schooling. *Journal of Applied Econometrics* 28(5):796–822

ESPAD (2015) *Report 2015. Results from the European School Survey Project on Alcohol and Other Drugs*. Luxembourg: Publications Office of the European Union

Fiorini M, Keane M (2014) How the allocation of children's time affects cognitive and noncognitive development. *Journal of Labor Economics* 32:787–836

Flèche S, Lekfuangfu WN, Clark AE (2021) The long-lasting effects of family and childhood on adult wellbeing. *Journal of Economic Behavior & Organization* 181:290–311

Fox L, Han WJ, Ruhm C, Waldfogel J. (2013) Time for children. *Demography* 50(1):25–49

Frey BS, Benesch C, Stutzer A (2007) Does watching TV make us happy? *Journal of Economic Psychology* 28(3):283–313

Fullerton AS, Wallace M (2007) Traversing the flexible turn. *Social Science Research* 36(1):201–221

Geishecker I (2010) Perceived job insecurity and well-being revisited. *SOEP Papers*, No. 282, https://papers.ssrn.com/sol3/papers.cfm?abstract_id=1577604

Givord P, Maurin E (2004) Changes in job security and their causes. *European Economic Review* 48:595–615

Gould ED, Hijzen A (2016) Growing apart, losing trust? *IMF Working Paper*, No. 16/176, Washington DC, https://www.imf.org/en/Publications/WP/Issues/2016/12/31/Growing-Apart-Losing-Trust-The-Impact-of-Inequality-on-Social-Capital-44197

Governo italiano (2017) *Relazione annuale al Parlamento 2017 sullo stato delle tossicodipendenza in Italia*. Roma: Dipartimento politiche antidroga

Green F (2009) Job quality in Britain. *Praxis*, No. 1. UK Commission for Employment and Skills, https://dera.ioe.ac.uk/1413/1/A5%20Job%20Quality%20in%20 Britain%20v6.pdf

Greitemeyer T, McLatchie N (2011) Denying humanness to others. *Psychological Science* 22:659–665

Gross DP (2018) Creativity under fire. *NBER Working Paper*, No. 25057. Cambridge, MA, https://www.nber.org/papers/w25057

Guryan J, Hurst E, Kearney M (2008) Parental education and parental time with children. *Journal of Economic Perspectives* 22(3):23–46

Guvenen F, Kaplan G, Song J, Weidner J (2017) Lifetime incomes in the United States over six decades. *NBER Working Paper*, No. 23371. Cambridge, MA, https://www. nber.org/papers/w23371

Hacker JS, Huber GA, Nichols A, Rehm P, Schlesinger M, Valletta R, Stuart C (2014) The economic security index. *Review of Income and Wealth* 60(S1):S5–S32

Hajdu G (2021). Perceived income inequality and subjective social status in Europe. *GLO Discussion Paper*, No. 926. Global Labor Organization, Essen

Hall KD, Guo J, Dore M, Chow CC (2009) The progressive increase of food waste in America and its environmental impact. *PLoS ONE* 4(11):e7940

Hamermesh DS, Lee J (2007) Stressed out on four continents. *Review of Economics and Statistics* 89(2):374–383

Hamermesh DS, Slemrod J (2008) The economics of workaholism. *The B.E. Journal of Economic Analysis & Policy* 8:1935–1682

Hanushek EA (2016) School human capital and teacher salary policies. *Journal of Professional Capital and Community* 1(1):23–40

Hanushek EA, Piopiunik M, Wiederhold S (2014) The value of smarter teachers. *NBER Working Paper*, No. 20727. Cambridge, MA, https://www.nber.org/papers/ w20727

Haslam N (2006) Dehumanization: An integrative review. *Personality and Social Psychology Review* 10:252–264

Hattie JAC (2003) Teachers make a difference: What is the research evidence? *ACER Research Conference*. Melbourne, Australia. Retrieved [23 Feb. 2022] from: http://research.acer.edu.au/research_conference_2003/4/

Heathcote J, Perri F, Violante GL (2020) The rise of US earnings inequality. *NBER Working Paper*, No. 23371. Cambridge, MA, http://www.nber.org/papers/w27345.pdf

Heckman JJ (2008) School, skills, and synapses. *Economic Inquiry* 46(3):289–324

Heckman JJ, Pinto R, Savelyev P (2013) Understanding the mechanisms through which an influential early childhood program boosted adult outcomes. *American Economic Review* 103(6):2052–2086

Heckman JJ, Stixrud J, Urzua S (2006) The effects of cognitive and noncognitive abilities on labour market outcomes and social behaviour. *Journal of Labour Economics* 24(3):411–482

Hoffman F, Lee DS, Lemieux T (2020) Growing income inequality in the United States and other advanced economies. *Journal of Economic Perspectives* 34(4):52–78

Hollister MN, Smith KE (2014) Unmasking the conflicting trends in job tenure by gender in the Unites States, 1983–2008. *American Sociological Review* 79(1):159–181

Hounkpatin HO, Wood AM, Brown GDA, Dunn G (2015) Why does income relate to depressive symptoms? *Social Indicators Research* 124:637–655

Hsin A, Felfe C (2014) When does time matter? *Demography* 51(5):1867–1894

Hyll W, Schneider L (2013) The causal effect of watching TV on material aspirations. *Journal of Economic Behavior & Organization* 86:37–51

James-Burdumy S (2005) The effect of maternal labor force participation on child development. *Journal of Labor Economics* 23:177–211

Jamieson PE, Romer D (2021) The association between the rise of gun violence in popular US primetime television dramas and homicides attributable to firearms, 2000–2018. *PLoS ONE* 16(3):e0247780

Judson E, Hobson A (2015) Growth and achievement trends of Advanced Placement exams in American high schools. *American Secondary Education* 43(2):59–76

Kambayashi R, Kato T (2017) Trends in long-term employment and job Security in Japan and the United States. *ILR Review* 70(2):359–394

Kashdan TB, Breen WE (2007) Materialism and diminished well-being. *Journal of Social and Clinical Psychology* 26(5):521–539

Katz LF, Krueger AB (2017) Documenting decline in U.S. economic mobility. *Science* 356(6336):382–383

Kautz T, Heckman JJ, Diris R, Weel BT, Borghans L (2014) Fostering and measuring skills. *OECD Education Working Papers*, No. 110. OECD Publishing, Paris

Kearney MS, Levine PB (2016) Income inequality, social mobility, and the decision to drop out of high school. *Brookings Papers on Economic Activity Spring* 2016:333–380

Keynes JM (1930) Economic possibilities for our grandchildren. In *Essays in Persuasion*. New York: W.W.Norton & Co., 1963, pp. 358–373

Kim KH (2011) The creativity crisis. *Creativity Research Journal* 23:1–11

Kim KH (2021) Creativity crisis update. *Roeper Review* 43:21–41

Knabe A, Raetzel S (2011) Scarring or scaring? The psychological impact of past unemployment and future unemployment risk. *Economica* 78(310):283–293

Konrath SH, O'Brien E, Hsing C (2011) Changes in dispositional empathy in American college students over time. *Personality and Social Psychology Review* 15:180–198

Kopasker D, Montagna C, Bender KA (2018) Economic insecurity. *Population Health* 6:184–194

Kroft K, Lange F, Notowidigdo MJ, Katz LF (2014) Long-term unemployment and the Great Recession. *NBER Working Paper*, No. 20273. Cambridge, MA, https://www.nber.org/papers/w20273

Kross E, Verduyn P, Demiralp E, Park J, Lee DS, et al. (2013) Facebook use predicts declines in subjective well-being in young adults. *PLoS ONE* 8(8):e69841

Krueger AB, Cramer J, Cho D (2014) Are the long-term unemployed margins of the labor market? In *Brookings Papers on Economic Activity*. Spring, Washington DC, pp. 229–280

Lane W, Sacco P, Downton K, Ludeman E, Levy L, Tracy JK (2016) Child maltreatment and problem gambling. *Child Abuse & Neglect* 58:24–38

Lavy V (2010) Do differences in schools' instruction time explain international achievement gaps? *NBER Working Paper*, No. 16227. Cambridge, MA, https://www.nber.org/papers/w16227

Layard R, Clark AE, Cornaglia F, Powdthavee N, Vernoit J (2014) What predicts a successful life? *Economic Journal* 124:F720–F738

Lee JO, Jones TM, Yoon Y, Hackman DA, Yoo JP, Kosterman R (2019) Young adult unemployment and later depression and anxiety. *Journal of Youth and Adolescence* 48(1):30–42

Lekfuangfu WN, Powdthavee N, Warrinnier N, Cornaglia F (2016) Locus of control and its intergenerational implications for early childhood skill formation. *Economic Journal* 128:298–329

LePera N (2011) Relationships between boredom proneness, mindfulness, anxiety, depression, and substance use. *New School Psychology Bulletin* 8(2):15–25

Løken K, Mogstad M, Wiswall M (2012) What linear estimation miss: The effects of family income on child outcomes. *American Economic Journal Applied Economics* 4(2):1–35

Lopes H, Calapez T, Lagoa S (2014) Work autonomy, work pressure and job satisfaction. *Economic and Labour Relations Review* 25:306–326

Lucas RE, Clark AE, Georgellis Y, Diener E (2004) Unemployment alters the set point for life satisfaction. *Psychological Science* 15(1):8–13

Luttmer E (2005) Neighbors as negatives. *Quarterly Journal of Economics* 120:963–1002

Macchia L, Oswald AJ (2021) Physical pain, gender, and economic trends in 146 nations. *Social Science & Medicine* 287(October):114332

Maclean JC, Mallatt J, Ruhm CM, Simon K (2020) Economic studies on the opioid crisis. *NBER Working Paper*, No. 28067. Cambridge, MA, https://www.nber.org/papers/w28067

Macload WB, Uequiola M (2019) Is education consumption or investment? *NBER Working Paper*, No. 25117. Cambridge, MA, https://www.nber.org/papers/w25117

Maslow A (1943) *Motivation and Personality*. Harper & Brothers, New York

Mikulincer M, Shaver PR (2007) *Attachment in Adulthood*. New York: Guilford Press

Montag C, Duke E, Reuter M (2015) A short summary of neuroscientific findings on internet addiction. In C Montag, E Duke, M Reuter (eds) *Internet Addiction*. Heidelberg: Springer, pp. 131–141

Moschion J, Powdthavee N (2017) The welfare implications of addictive substances. *IZA DP* 11181

Mujcic R, Oswald AJ (2018) Is envy harmful to a society's psychological health and wellbeing?, *Social Science & Medicine* 198:103–111

Neidell MJ (2000) Early parental time investments in children's human capital development. *UCLA wp* 806, http://www.econ.ucla.edu/workingpapers/wp806.pdf

Odermatt R, Stutzer A (2015) Smoking bans, cigarette prices and life satisfaction. *Journal of Health Economics* 44:176–194

OECD (2015) *Students, Computers and Learning*. Paris: OECD Publishing

Oishi S, Kesebir S, Diener E (2011) Income inequality and happiness. *Psychological Science* 22(9):1095–1100

Oliverio A (2008) Brain and creativity. *Progress of Theoretical Physics Supplement* 173:66–78

ONS – Office for National Statistics (2017) Deaths related to drug poisoning in England and Wales: 2016 registration. *Statistical Bulletin*. Release 2 August 2017

Oreopoulos P, von Wachter T, Heisz A (2012) The short- and long-term career effects of graduating in a recession. *American Economic Journal* 4(1):1–29

Oreopoulos P, Petronijevic U (2014) Making college worth it. *NBER Working Paper*, No. 19053. Cambridge, MA, https://www.nber.org/papers/w19053

Orru K, Orru H, Maasikmets M, Hendrikson R, Ainsaar M (2016) Well-being and environmental quality. *Quality of Life Research* 25(3):699–705

Otterbach S, Souza-Poza A (2016) Job insecurity, employability, and health. *Applied Economics* 48(14):1303–1316

Pénard M, Mayol T (2017) Facebook use and individual well-being. *Revue d'économie industrielle* 158:101–127

Piaget J (1973) *To Understand is to Invent*. Viking, New York

Pickett KE, Wilkinson RG (2015) Income inequality and health. *Social Science & Medicine* 128:316–326

Popovici I, French MT (2013) Does unemployment lead to greater alcohol consumption? *Industrial Relations* 52(2):444–466

Powdthavee N (2014) What childhood characteristics predict psychological resilience to economic shocks in adulthood? *Journal of Economic Psychology* 45:84–101

Przybylski AK, Weinstein N (2017) A large-scale test of the goldilocks hypothesis. *Psychological Science* 28:2014–2015

Pudney S (2004) Keeping off the grass? *Journal of Applied Econometrics* 19:435–453

Pugno M (2009) The Easterlin paradox and the decline of social capital. *Journal of Socio-Economics* 38(4):590–600

Pugno M, Sarracino F (2021) Intrinsic vs extrinsic motivation to protect the environment. *MPRA Paper*, No. 107143, https://mpra.ub.uni-muenchen.de/107143/1/MPRA_paper_107143.pdf

Ramey G, Ramey VA (2010) The rug rat race. In *Brookings Papers on Economic Activity*. Washington DC, Spring, pp. 129–176

Rao H, Betancourt L, Giannetta JM, et al. (2010) Early parental care is important for hippocampal maturation. *NeuroImage* 49(1):1144–1150

Reardon SF, Valentino RA, Shores KA (2012) Patterns of literacy among U.S. students. *The Future of Children* 22(2):17–38

Robins LN, Slobodyan S (2003) Post-Vietnam heroin use and injection by returning US veterans. *Addiction* 98(8):1053–1060

Rockloff MJ, Greer N, Fay C, Evans LG (2011) Gambling on electronic gaming machines is an escape from negative self reflection. *Journal of Gambling Studies* 27:63–72

Ross D (2010) Book review. *Journal of Economic Psychology* 31:146–148

Ruhm C (2018). Deaths of despair or drug problems? *NBER Working Paper*, No. 24188. Cambridge, MA, https://www.nber.org/papers/w24188

Sabatini F, Sarracino F (2017) Online social networks and well-being. *Kyklos* 70:465–480

Sayer LC, Gornick JC (2012) Cross-national variation in the influence of employment hours on child care time. *European Sociological Review* 28(4):421–442

Schwandt H, von Wachter TM (2019) Unlucky cohorts. *NBER Working Paper*, No. 25141. Cambridge, MA, https://www.nber.org/papers/w25141

Schwandt H, von Wachter TM (2020) Socioeconomic Decline and death. *IZA DP*, No. 12908, https://docs.iza.org/dp12908.pdf

Sevilla A, Gimenez-Nadal JI, Gershuny J (2012) Leisure inequality in the United States. *Demography* 49(3):939–964

Sheldon KM, Kasser T (2008). Psychological threat and extrinsic goal striving. *Motivation and Emotion* 32:37–45

Siddique AB (2021) *Poverty in the USA*. Retrieved [22 Feb. 2022] from: https://ssrn.com/abstract=3808725

Spichtig AN, Hiebert EH, Vorstius C, et al (2016) The decline of comprehension-based silent reading efficiency in the United States. *Reading Research Quarterly* 51(2):239–259

Stiglitz JE (2008) Toward a general theory of consumerism. In L Pecchi, G Piga (eds) *Revisiting Keynes*. Cambridge, MA: MIT Press, pp. 41–86

Stiglitz JE (2012) Macroeconomic fluctuations, inequality, and human development. *Journal of Human Development and Capabilities* 13(1):31–58

Stuhler JA (2018) *Review of Intergenerational Mobility and its Drivers*. Luxembourg: Publications Office of the European Union

Sung Y, Nam T-H, Hwang MH (2020) Attachment style, stressful events, and Internet gaming addiction in Korean university students. *Personality and Individual Differences* 154(1):109724

Tay L, Diener E (2011) Needs and subjective well-being around the world. *Journal of Personality and Social Psychology* 101(2):354–365

Tromholt M (2016) The Facebook experiment. *Cyberpsychology, Behavior, and Social Networking* 19(11):661–666

Turkle S (2011) *Alone Together*. Basic Books, New York

Twenge M, Campbell SM, Hoffman BJ, Lance CE (2010) Generational differences in work values. *Journal of Management* 36:1117–1142

Twenge JM, Campbell WK, Freeman EC (2012) Generational differences in young adults' life goals, concern for others, and civic orientation. *Journal of Personality and Social Psychology* 102(5):1045–1062

Twenge JM, Campbell WK, Carter NT (2014) Declines in trust in others and confidence in institutions among American adults and late adolescents. *Psychological Science* 25(10):1914–1923

Twenge JM, Joiner TE, Rogers ML (2018) Increases in depressive symptoms, suicide-related outcomes, and suicide rates among U.S. adolescents after 2010 and links to increased new media screen time. *Clinical Psychological Science* 6(1):3–17

Twenge JM, Zhang L, Im C (2004) Beyond my control. *Personality and Social Psychology Review* 8(3):308–319

van Deurzen IA, van Ingen EJ, van Oorschot WJH (2015) Income inequality and depression. *European Sociological Review* 31(4):477–489

Vygotsky L (1978[1930]) *Mind and Society*. Cambridge, MA: Harvard University Press

Wolff EN, Baumol WJ, Saini AN (2014) A comparative analysis of education costs and outcomes. *Economics of Education* 39:1–21

Wright EO, Dwyer R (2003) The patterns of job expansions in the USA. *Socio-Economic Review* 1:289–325

4 Economic growth and human development
Which priority in the post-pandemic era?

4.1 The COVID-19 pandemic: hindrance or opportunity for human development?

The Great Recession of 2008–2009 was a stress test for economies, including advanced economies. It was the biggest economic shock since the Great Depression of the 1930s. However, unlike that distant dramatic experience, the Great Recession was not taken as an opportunity to radically change the traditional role assigned to the markets as the engine of economic growth. To seriously question this conventional wisdom came the shock of the COVID-19 pandemic, even more violent in hitting the economy and more direct in disrupting the daily lives of the entire population.

The pandemic that broke out at the turn of 2019–2020 was in fact unique in terms of the speed of spread and the global extent of the impact, and now it is even unknown when it will become irrelevant. Governments have responded, albeit differently from country to country, by taking a series of exceptional measures to alleviate the consequences of the shock. In a long-run perspective, the problem then becomes whether individuals and governments take the opportunity to re-think the priorities in their choices and policies and in particular whether economic growth is maintained as the priority.

Unfortunately, a number of premises do not bode well. First, the pandemic has greatly increased people's insecurity, not only for their own health but also for economic reasons. Employment has been threatened by the violent cyclical instability due to the pandemic shock, by the technological leap of labour replacement due to precautionary social distancing, and by sectoral restructuring due to the different composition of private and public demand. Another source of insecurity stemming from the pandemic has been the greater inequality in the labour market, in schools, and in access to public health services.[1] The need to alleviate insecurity has thus become more pervasive and urgent, and this concern is a bad premise for people to pursue more ambitious goals in their lives.

DOI: 10.4324/9781003241676-6

Second, the pandemic has hindered people from performing some fundamental activities for their human development, namely education and cultural activities with direct social contact, while it has favoured spending time with high-tech consumer products. In many cases, in fact, the pandemic has forced educational activities to shift from face-to-face interaction to online education, which is less effective, especially in first grades but also at university (Altindag et al. 2021; Donnelly & Patrinos 2021). A study focused on the primary schools in the Netherlands, which is the country with the world's highest rate of broadband access, estimates that 8 weeks of lockdown result in a learning loss of 0.08 standard deviation, implying that students made very little progress while learning from home (Engzell et al. 2021). Another study from the United Kingdom (UK) revealed that students have more than halved their learning time during closures compared with before and have partially replaced it with computer gaming, social media, and watching television (Grewenig et al. 2020).

Along with the restrictions on social distancing and limited economic activity, many cultural events, exhibitions, concerts, performances, and festivals have been cancelled, with negative effects on cultural workers, freelancers, the self-employed, and other stakeholders in the so-called 'creative sector'. The use of the digital technologies has thus become more widespread when possible (Khlystova et al. 2021).

In the case of education and other socio-cultural activities, the consequences of the pandemic shock are long run because they involve changes in people's preferences and in the productive organisation of many services. A study of the World Bank predicts that "school closures could result in a loss of between 0.3 and 1.1 years of schooling adjusted for quality", with negative consequences on lifetime earnings and health (Azevedo et al. 2021:1). On the production side, the rapid diffusion of high-tech communication products has already strengthened the industrial concentration (Chattergoon & Kerr 2021; Valero et al. 2021).

Third, the pandemic has deteriorated, on average, people's mental health because risk factors, such as financial insecurity, unemployment, and fear of infection, have increased, whereas protective factors, such as employment, social connection, education engagement, and access to health services, have decreased. Despite the limited availability of reliable and updated measures for people's mental health, a variety of indicators point in the same worrying direction: in the United States (US), the deaths due to drug overdose, suicide, and alcohol, called 'deaths of despair', increased in 2020 (Mulligan 2020; see also Queadan et al. 2021); COVID-symptoms and COVID-based life changes are closely correlated with moderate to severe depression and anxiety symptoms, especially in the advanced set of countries; the moderate to severe depression and anxiety symptoms have increased during the lockdown in Italy; and mild mental health problems worsened in a panel of representative sample of the UK from 2019 to 2020.[2]

An editorial of a scientific psychology journal warned that the COVID-19 pandemic has revealed the other pandemic of mental disorders. In fact, it observed that "as of August 24th, 2020, COVID-19 had caused 800,000 deaths worldwide. This is precisely the same number of people who commit suicide every year. The difference is that COVID-19 will likely have an end, either through a vaccine or through eventual mass immunity. The mental health crisis may very well continue" (Swendsen 2020:162), the reason being that social determinants play a key role (OECD 2021; *Lancet* 2021). What remains unclear is whether the COVID-19 pandemic has contributed to a *permanent* aggravation of people's mental problems, both moderate and severe.

Fourth, the anti-pandemic restrictions imposed by governments and local authorities, along with the vaccination campaign, have exacerbated the social divides that have already emerged with the surge in demand for populist and nationalistic policies (Lackner et al. 2021) (see Chapter 1). In particular, the belief that the so-called 'elite' controls 'the people' to better protect its interest is reinforced with the suspicion that vaccines are a special means of control. This prompts people opposing vaccination to harshly confront those in favour, far beyond a science-based controversy. The suspicion that Chinese and immigrants were responsible for the pandemic further reinforces racial animosity.

This can be clearly confirmed by looking again at the two cases of Trump supporters and of voters for Brexit. People living in US counties where Trump found strong support for his 2016 presidential election are less likely to wear virus masks (Kahane 2021). More generally, a significant gap has arisen between Republicans and Democrats in beliefs about the severity of COVID-19 and the importance of social distancing, having taken into account the population density, cases, and deaths from COVID-19 (Allcott et al. 2020). A causal analysis has further shown that the gap has been driven by the earlier animus in partisan polarisation (Druckman et al. 2021). A clear confirmation for the Brexit case comes from the close relationship between the 2016 Brexit vote and COVID-19 death, infection, and vaccination rates in England (Phalippou & Wu 2021).

With regard to racism, a study based on Google searches and Twitter posts finds that the COVID-19 pandemic has led to a surge in racial animus against Asians, as a prelude to racial hate crimes, especially when Trump has posted tweets mentioning China and COVID-19 at the same time (Lu & Sheng 2020). Analogously, a study based on a large sample of UK citizens finds that COVID-19 has exacerbated anti-immigrant attitudes among leavers in the Brexit referendum while having little effect on remainers (Pickup et al. 2021).

The shock of the pandemic is thus likely to have very prolonged effects through the consolidation of identities in social groups and through the social division between those who contributed to dampen the pandemic by taking the vaccine and those who did not. For example, hesitancy in taking the vaccine only partially decreased in the first 3 months of vaccination in the US despite the great amount of deaths from COVID-19 (Beleche et al. 2021), and this would prevent herd immunity from being achieved, with prolonged dramatic consequences (Dabla-Norris et al. 2021). A further effect of the pandemic shock is the drop of trust in democracy, even in the advanced countries (Becher et al. 2021). Looking at past experiences of pandemic, we could even expect social unrest, although not in the immediate future (Barrett & Chen 2021).

Fortunately, the COVID-19 pandemic has not only brought problems; it has also highlighted *opportunities* to improve people's lives with respect to the past. Specifically, people may have recognised the importance of the fundamental human capability, that is, creativity-and-sociality as we have define it, thus taking the first step in resetting the priority in life goals.

Regarding *sociality*, the pandemic has highlighted the importance of social interdependence, which has been overshadowed by economic interdependence. Indeed, agents in the market are interdependent because they are interested in the exchange of goods and services, whereas people in personal relationships maintain an intrinsic interest in their partners. Machines offer great possibilities for enhancing economic interdependence, whereas they offer connections that are poor substitutes for direct personal contacts in social interdependence. The lockdowns and social distance during the pandemic have highlighted the importance of direct personal contacts and the poor performance, albeit often valuable, of distance communication technologies.[3]

The typical case is schooling. As never before during the pandemic, the school has been at the centre of public debate. Educators have expressed great concern about school closures and the limits of distance learning. Students often complained that they could not study with their classmates. Governments have often maintained a strong focus on school attendance during the pandemic. Hence, this may be the right time to permanently devote more resources to the schools.

But the COVID-19 infection among people, also when they do not know one another, has made the argument for social interdependence even stronger. The individual decision to protect themselves with anti-virus masks and vaccinations is combined with the protection of others. And the more unprotected people there are, the higher the probability of virus mutation, and the persistence of the pandemic. Since protective measures limit some liberties, and vaccination is not completely free from health risks, the pandemic has reminded us that belonging to the same human species imposes some duty on us. Therefore, different from the case of the market, a central coordination among individuals is required to counter the pandemic. A lesson then follows to strengthen public intervention to prevent and deal with any future similar eventualities.

Realising that the health of people has also the characteristics of the public good could strengthen the consensus to take a central action to preserve and dealing with another public good: the natural environment. Indeed, going through the disastrous global experience of the pandemic reveals how insufficient individual-based forces would be to escape the expected worsening of environmental degradation.

Regarding *creativity*, the impact of the pandemic is more intriguing and with possible beneficial consequences in the future. The shock of the pandemic has been so global and severe that it has revealed the vulnerability of human life but also the vulnerability of entire economies, even advanced economies. This fact forces people and governments to imagine a future different from the recent pre-pandemic past and thus to wonder what to do to improve it. People may become more creative as they re-focus on their aspirations and hence on their ability to control the way to achieve them in adherence with their abilities, social context, and economic opportunities. Governments may become more creative as they are urged to re-conceive their intervention in the economy to prevent disasters affecting the population, as in the case of the European Union.

Therefore, the pandemic has brought us many problems and some opportunities, and this further complicates the re-prioritisation of people's choices and government policies. A complex strategy of interventions is thus necessary to displace economic growth from the top priority and make it functional to human development.

4.2 Prioritising human development: how to relax its constrains

Actions to make effective the priority of human development as an expansion of the fundamental capability in people's choices and governments' policies need a strategy. In fact, the conditions under which the actions should be applied are progressively consolidating in a complex and unfavourable way. A comprehensive strategy includes three sets of synergistic actions: the first one should relax the constraints on human development, the second should directly promote human development, and the third should defend human development from those market (and non-market) forces that press in the opposite direction. Let us see them in turn in this and the next two sections, respectively. Rather than listing and discussing in detail all the required interventions, however, we will pay attention to how the strategy should work, thus suggesting a way to organise scattered and sometimes well-known pre-scriptions in relation to our unique concept of human development.

The first group of actions should relax the constraints on human devel-opment, which are perceived by people as problems of greatest concern, making the future very uncertain. In fact, to alleviate such problems, people devote most of their resources, including time and effort, and cease to think about their future by being focused on the present.

The constraints on human development can be 'external' or 'internal' to individuals. The 'external' constraints are mainly due to economic depri-vations in terms of lack of income, wealth, and work. *Absolute economic deprivation* refers to the case of poverty when this is below the subsistence level, sometimes experienced after prolonged or recurrent unemployment. In this case, the primary proper action is obviously to provide public subsi-dies and proper care to people with such needs.

The relative economic deprivation is a more complex problem instead. The *deprivation relative to others* is a reflection of the economic inequal-ity that has soared in the past decades even within advanced countries. For everyone to have their own human development, the goal is 'equality of opportunity', meaning the equality of chances for everyone at the begin-ning of their lives. The equalisation of economic conditions that alter the opportunities faced by the individuals strongly suggests providing all citi-zens with public services, such as health care, education, housing, and urban transport, at very low price for people. Another policy with the same goal is to levy a proper inheritance tax, accompanied by more progressive taxation (Piketty & Saez 2013).

The *deprivation relative to the past* is due to cyclical recessions or to sec-toral declines for productive restructuring, which are more likely when the trend of economic growth decelerates. The need for much-debated policies finds a rationale here. Worth mentioning are anti-cyclical policies, legislation to protect workers (rather than jobs), industrial policy to orient technological progress and help economic growth,[4] and regulation of financial markets to discourage bubbles and the excessive conditioning of other policies.[5]

The 'internal' constraints to individuals are due to the lack of health, both physical and mental. Indeed, diseases and malaise can compromise or alter individuals' performance in any activity, relationships with others, and any form of cooperation. The alteration can be immediate or persist even for the entire life-cycle. In particular, mental health problems often remain at subclinical levels, thus hindering their diagnosis and demand for their treat-ment. Consequently, the prevalence of mental illness in its varying degrees of severity is underestimated, and the mental health services are under-funded even in the advanced countries. Despite this, overall health services greatly suffer from soaring costs for both the public budget and households.

One way to improve the effectiveness of population health care and to limit health care costs is to extend the focus from specific diseases, which is the current trend, to the general health status of patients. This requires strengthening the monitoring and the first taking charge of the population through the territorial health services, especially in schools and neighbourhoods. Teams of community doctors should include psychologists, besides general practitioners and paediatricians. Investing in health workers for disease prevention, early care, and education for healthy lifestyles could save medicines, clinical exams, and hospital admissions.

To clarify these last aspects, some numbers may be useful. Expenditure on the treatment of people with 'mental disorders' as a whole accounts for only 15% of health expenditure in Europe even though these illnesses directly affect more than a quarter of the population and are some of the main causes of mortality and disability, resulting in health, social, and economic costs estimated at around 4% of gross domestic product (Andlin-Sobocki et al. 2005; see also Wittchen et al. 2015). These (indirect) costs plus the (direct) costs to cure mental disorders are higher than those of the physical diseases, but their treatment has a higher benefit-to-cost ratio (Trautmann et al. 2016).

Relaxing these constraints on human development, however, is not sufficient. Alleviating economic deprivations, both absolute and relative, does not guarantee that individuals use their new resources for their human development rather than for other goals that could displace it. Keynes mentioned in 1930 one of such goals as money-making per se, which cannot be said to have disappeared even in our times (Keynes 1930).[6] Alleviating the problems of health does not guarantee that individuals use their newfound energy and time to maximise their human development.[7] Alleviating ill-beings arising from economic and health concerns does not ensure well-being, since ill-being and well-being are not symmetrical and since absence of concerns does not imply that people then thrive.

Therefore, more targeted actions are necessary to promote human development.

4.3 Prioritising human development: how to directly promote it

The second group of actions should directly promote human development by stimulating people's capability of creativity-and-sociality. Even when economic and health deprivations were substantially absent, this capability could be weak, overlooked, deteriorated, or even latent. The direct promotion of human development by both individuals and institutions means choosing and organising activities that require the exercise of the fundamental capability, such as stimulating curiosity, taking on challenges, exchanging ideas with others, or collaborating on common projects. The possible rediscover and then the exercise of this capability, in fact, have the property of triggering and nourishing human development as a self-generating process. People can thus become freer both to do and to be but in a direction that guarantees individual and social well-being.

The choices and policies that directly promote human development concern three domains in people's lives: education, including early education; work; and, in strict connection, free time (Pugno 2016b; Pugno & Depedri 2010).

The primary domain for promoting human development is *education*. The current educational practice in advanced countries, however, is not designed for such purpose, so it is inefficient at best or perverse at worst. The usual practice in early education is to leave parents with complete discretion in their educational role as if children were private consumption or investment goods.[8] Then, the school system is designed to transfer a somewhat uniform stock of knowledge to children and adolescents and to motivate them to absorb that knowledge through competition in the expectation of finding better jobs. In tertiary education, competition becomes even fiercer, and this requires increasing financial and educational support from parents. The result is that students' interest in learning has decreased (OECD 2017:119; Högberg et al. 2018), and the work of educators has become less attractive (see Chapter 3).

Changing the current educational practice is difficult because it is based on the widespread belief that creativity is a gift for the few and that sociality is only useful for taking care of others' needs while it generally dampens the individual motivation to make productive efforts. Authoritative studies rather show that the opposite is true (see Chapter 3). Creativity can be effectively stimulated not only in early childhood but also in later years.[9] Socio-emotional skills are more plastic than cognitive skills since early adolescence, and help individuals in achieving better outcomes at schools and at work (Borghans et al. 2008).

Fortunately, alternative educational practices have already been conceived and experimented with success around the world. For example, the Montessori programme of education, which is characterised by multi-age classrooms, a stimulating set of educational materials, individual and small group instruction, collaboration, and an absence of grades and tests, has been adopted in several primary and elementary schools with success. In fact, students in this programme reveal more creativity-and-sociality than the other students (Lillard & Else-Quest 2006). The obvious implication is to advice parents to learn how to educate their children from programmes like these, and educational authorities to also adopt similar programmes.[10]

The key ingredients of these programmes should be the time invested in face-to-face interaction[11] and the ability of educators to stimulate the exercise of children's creativity-and-sociality. Around these two ingredients, the educational system should be organised, and technology for education should be used.

Changing educational programmes, however, are not sufficient. Family background and geographic location also play a role, besides children's original talents, so that policies to provide educational supports to families and to encourage geographical mobility and desegregation are necessary to make those programmes as effective. While the research in the economic literature on the effectiveness of educational support for disadvantaged families has become extensive and rigorous (Garcìa et al. 2016), the research on the need for greater geographical mobility is less sought after, but some economic studies already provide interesting results. They show that children whose families move to high-innovation areas are more likely to become creative, measured with patenting, thus making it clear how social networks can enhance individual education (Bell et al. 2019).

This means that education for human development based of the fundamental capability requires a set of coordinated policies. A special advantage of such policies is to reveal and then develop talents in people which would have remained latent or frustrated, that is – one could say – to uncover latent Einsteins.

The other two main domains for promoting human development in people's lives are *work* and *free time*. Unfortunately, market forces go in a rather different direction that people have not found difficult to follow. In fact, producers buy people's working time and effort for the goal of making profit, and people sell time and effort in exchange for income. In other words, market forces tend to persuade people to maintain the pattern that 'work is the necessary pain to earn subsistence' even if a century of productivity growth would have made this obsolete for most of the population, at least in advanced countries. Indeed, the advance of technology has made it possible to reduce working time and physical effort, but it has also enabled producers to offer such attractive quantity and quality of goods that many luxuries have become necessary, and the new free time has remained leisure, that is, time for rest, consume, and fleeting fun.

However, increasing evidence reveal that work has important nonmonetary returns, thus showing that there is room for promoting human development in this domain. By investigating what makes work satisfying, different studies find that pay and job security provide only a partial answer, which should be supplemented with nonmonetary returns, such as 'meaning', 'purpose', 'interest, 'interpersonal relationships', challenging competence, or 'work identity' (Cassar & Meier 2018; Krekel et al. 2019; Nikolova & Femke 2020; Bryan & Nandi 2015).

Promoting human development at work requires that businesses, workers, customers, and the public sector interact to achieve the common purpose to improve workers' capability of creativity-and-sociality subject to the constraint of environmental conservation. Businesses should forgo making the most of workers' time and effort (as well as non-renewable resource inputs) while taking advantage of workers' motivation and creativity (Amabile et al. 2005) and of innovations provided by proper public investment. To these ends, workers should participate in business decisions, the public sector should organise and support missions for business (Mazzucato 2011), and consumers should prefer goods and services that respect workers and the environment.

People who have the possibility to enjoy such favourable working conditions for human development can also live their free time differently. Since the achievements and even the effort at work are pleasant, they do not need to spend free time and to consume goods as self-medication. On the contrary, the things learned at work, the ideas exchanged with colleagues, and the renewed energies in the pursuit of work projects can spill over the free time activities, thus adjusting the consumption basket accordingly.

People, who have *fewer* possibilities to enjoy such favourable conditions for human development at work, essentially because of their initial skills and socio-economic background, should find more opportunities in their free time. The associations that organise social, cultural, sporting, and pro-environmental activities already offer a range of opportunities (Lawton et al. 2020), but they should multiply and grow by renovating traditional or local resources, up to the point of confrontation and interaction with market activities. These associations can also become a training ground for elaborating consensus useful for orienting policies and making them effective.

In particular, cultural policy, which is especially important to human development, could rely less on subsidies for cultural activities at risk of disappearing from the market due to the well-known law of Baumol's cost disease. Not only can educational policy for human development provide greater demand for cultural activities, but the rise of local cultural associations can also help new developments of cultural activities in a possible interaction with the market (van der Ploeg 2006; Blessi et al. 2014).

All these actions to promote human development even in combination with actions to relax the constraints on human development, however, may not be sufficient. In fact, market forces empowered by the recent concentration of new high-technology services press to manipulate individuals' preferences and beliefs and to alter policies. This calls for an active defence of human development.

4.4   Prioritising human development: how to defend it

Human development, as we have defined it, is the development of the twofold fundamental human capability of creativity-and-sociality. By creativity, we mean the ability to create new knowledge, as abstract ideas or material innovations, about oneself, about the relationship with others, or about the natural world. Being creative implies being able to conceive *new goals*, which appear attractive because they are challenging and enjoyable in their pursuit. Creativity reinforces itself through its exercise, thus displaying *internalities*, which are inner outcomes imperfectly foreseen, such as changes in individuals' preferences and beliefs. By sociality, we mean the ability to interact with others to achieve *common goals*. Both in interpersonal relationships and in drawing from or contributing to the societal stock of knowledge, sociality displays *externalities* (see also Chapter 2).

Economic growth is expected to provide more resources for more ambitious goals and multiplied opportunities for societal collaboration. The market should let individuals freely choose what is best for them, while the state may appear to be the only threat to individual freedom by imposing taxes and regulations. However, as we have already seen in Chapter 3, economic growth driven by market expansion is not so neutral. In fact, it typically gives rise to cyclical instability and economic inequality, which tend to heavily condition individuals' goals and collaboration, while the greater quantity and quality of market products at relatively lower prices tend to attract individuals' preferences by forming habits and addictions, thus displacing human development. The recent concentration of new high-tech services, which include digital platforms and its integration with logistics, is becoming an additional market force that conditions individuals with greater pressure and is even able of conditioning governments (Zuboff 2019; Coveri et al. 2021).

Our argument in a nutshell is that the system of digital platforms, led by corporations such as Facebook, Google, and Amazon, is altering individuals' internalities and societal externalities because the goal of maximising platforms' profits tends to prevail over the personal goals of their customers, thus threatening human development. A side conclusion is that the market cannot be seen in opposition to the state because both of them influence the choices of individuals.

Platforms mediate buyers and sellers, workers and employers, advertisers and consumers by using digital networks, data storage, cloud computing, artificial intelligence, and machine learning. Since platforms own and control the data, they dictate the terms of the interactions. Since customers' advantage in using this type of service depends on their number, platforms can exploit so large economies of scale that they become quasi-monopolistic. Since digital technology is extremely versatile and can be easily miniaturised, platforms tend to offer services for every human activity (Kenney & Zysman 2016).

The use of platform services thus becomes an increasingly forced choice to interact with others, and this has deleterious consequences (provided that human development has already some weaknesses). For example, popular platforms offer subscribers the free possibility to publish pictures and texts describing personal daily experiences and possessions, with the effect of spreading comparisons among viewers. In this case, the externality takes the forms of personal competition, thus mimicking market competition, and of social conformism, thus frustrating innovative ideas. Both of them further weaken individuals' human development. Another example is the possibility to search information made incredibly easy and extensive by some platforms, with the unsolicited consequence of receiving advertisements and selected information on the same product and topic of the original search. Over time, the pressure initially coming from producers can become pressure from peers, thus bringing preferences and beliefs to conformism, further weakening individuals' internality and human development.[12]

The immediate goal of platforms is to appropriate and control personal data from customers to accumulate a formidable stock of intangible capital. This stock can be mainly used to persuade consumers buying market products through advertising, to instruct artificial intelligence, to influence voters in political elections. Therefore, the goal of platforms is likely to diverge from customers' goals, with the aggravating factor that the use of personal data remains largely unknown and beyond customers' control. For example, people would welcome to use their data for research in preventive health rather than mapping population's political profiles.

Other hindrances to people's human development coming from digital platforms relate to the labour market. It is undeniable that platforms have led to the fragmentation and precariousness of work, task surveillance, conflict with trade unions, and the hiring of the most innovative workers to either exploit their ideas for commercial goals or prevent dangerous competition. In so doing, platforms have led greater insecurity in individuals and income inequality in society (Zuboff 2019).

Even at the government level, the impact of platforms has had deleterious effects. Their financial power has grown so much that the single platform is able to pay lobbyists and lawyers with a past political career to condition governments in their favour in anti-trust law, labour policy, and fiscal policy. And the dependence of consumers on their services provides them with a broad basis of consensus (Coveri 2021).

In the face of such powerful forces of platforms, the defence of people's human development requires intervening in their own playing field. Public enterprises should provide platform services but with all the desirable guarantees, such as privacy protection, retention of propriety of personal data, ethical principles, removal of hate speech, data collection, processing, and storage procedures. Their goals should be democratically discussed with competent committees, and their action should be mission orientated with adequate budget and management. Services could focus on sectors that private platforms find unprofitable or risky, such as education, health, the organisation of cultural associations, neighbourhood communities, pro-environmental activities, or promotion of social innovations. If their missions are explicit and with both scientific and popular consensus, public platforms can become competitive thanks to the widespread collaboration of the population in offering personal data. A further advantage of public platforms is the possibility of interacting with public research centres, including universities, which can be properly funded for both basic and applied research.[13]

From this position of strength, it becomes easier enact new legislation on digital platforms inspired from two basic principles. First, people should be better protected in their rights, as consumers, as workers, and as producers, from the pervasive force of private platforms, for example, by restricting advertising and contract work. Second, knowledge, including innovative knowledge, should be made more easily accessible, for example, by liberalising private intellectual property rights and by forcing private platforms to be more transparent in their use of data (Dosi & Virgillito 2019).

Unfortunately, people's human development should not only be defended from private digital platforms but also from an old threat. As the war in Ukraine painfully reminds us, a dangerous threat comes when democracy is attacked or, as in the case of social divides and nationalism, when democracy is worn down. Indeed, the loss of freedom and confidence in institutions can seriously hinder human development.

4.5 How human development can change the pattern of economic growth

One would expect that prioritising fundamental human development over economic growth in people's choices and governments' policies necessarily implies a reduction in the rate of economic growth. The reasons are that generous public services, pro-environmental policies, and redistributive actions in favour to poorer and unemployed people, as well as greater participation in decision-making processes are costly. However, the negative implication on economic growth is not necessary because its pattern, in terms of structure, equality, and employment, will improve, with positive effects on its speed. Let us briefly see how these results could be achieved.

Prioritising human development primarily suggests investing in early education, namely, when individuals' capability of creativity-and-sociality arises and can most develop. According to James Heckman, investing in early education when children live in disadvantaged conditions can improve not only social equity but also economic efficiency, thus contravening the standard problem of trade-off (Heckman 2008). Such an investment yields a so high rate of return that it is very cost-effective. Heckman insists on the fact that non-cognitive skills, such as the internal locus of control and self-esteem, are more malleable than cognitive skills and that both of them contribute to better academic achievement, to avoid anti-social behaviours, to find a job, and to earn a higher wage in later ages (Heckman et al. 2006; see also Deming 2017).

In the case of schools teaching practices that pay more attention to students' creativity-and-sociality, their experience can provide useful inputs for the economy. This emerges clearly from the following examples. A preliminary study shows that an alternative teaching practice to the traditional lecture because organised on group work is sufficient to observe in students a greater general trust, civic participation, and self-confidence (Algan et al. 2013). Then, according to other studies, general trust, cooperative belief and participation in associations engaged in social welfare, youth work, cultural activities, and the environment have positive effects on economic growth. The reason is that transactions, agreements, risk-taking, and decentralisation of decisions within firms become easier (Algan et al. 2014; Muringani et al. 2021). Still other studies show that people who have a greater internal locus of control are more likely to engage in general vocational training, have higher reservation wages when they search for a job (Caliendo et al. 2020, 2015), demand less employment protection legislation (D'Orlando et al. 2011), have greater motivation to become entrepreneurs, and are correlated to the size and growth rates of their enterprises (Kurjono 2018; Kerr et al. 2017).

Investing in education to stimulate the participation of the entire school-age population (and beyond) makes it possible to discover latent talents and to take advantage of everyone's capabilities, with benefits for economic growth and social cohesion. To give an idea, it has been calculated, for the case of the United States, that the extension to women and Black people of the free possibility to participate in education from the levels of 1960 to those of 2010 accounted for one-quarter of the economic growth per-capita (Hsieh et al. 2019).

Prioritising human development could even benefit work performance. In general, when individuals choose to exercise the capability of creativity-and-sociality, they are intrinsically motivated, that is, they expect higher well-being both in such exercise and in its outcome relatively to alternative choices. In the case of work, individuals are intrinsically motivated when they enjoy challenging their skills in dealing with open problems, thus generally involving the search for new and more efficient combinations of productive inputs.

There are several pieces of supporting evidence on this issue, coming from different disciplines. A general finding is that intrinsic motivation contributes positively to work performance. In particular, the contribution of intrinsic motivation seems greater than that of extrinsic motivation,[14] especially when tasks require intuition and careful thought (Kuvaas 2018; Pugno & Depedri 2010; Camerer & Hogarth 1999; Weibel et al. 2007). Psychological studies stress that intrinsic motivation is linked to creativity and that creativity is a prerequisite of innovations in productive organisations and thus important for their success on the market (Anderson et al. 2013). Experimental studies in economics show that general trust and team cooperation facilitate creativity (Attanasi et al. 2021).

Intrinsic motivation as part of human development contributes positively to work performance, especially for its creativity component. However, – as Teresa Amabile argues in her article "How to kill creativity", – "creativity is undermined unintentionally every day in work environments that were established to maximize business imperatives such as co-ordination, productivity, and control" (Amabile 1998:18). The problem is that the proportion of executive and routine tasks is still great, and this must be as predictable as possible, thus leaving no room for creative action. But machines should be called for to substitute for workers in such type of tasks, as has happened many times in the history of industrialisation.

The problem thus becomes technological unemployment, that is, how to manage workers substituted by machines. Unemployment benefit and the reduction of working hours are often invoked as remedies, but they are not without drawbacks. Indeed, displaced workers, especially men, often suffer the stigma of being unemployed, and the preference for longer working hours prevails. The exit strategy from this problem is human development because it could turn the job position of workers as threatened by machines into a synergistic relationship with them and because human development enables people to find life goals in which work is a complementary possibility to pursue them. To better reconcile such renovated balance between work and private life, greater work flexibility should be properly designed and introduced.

Intrinsic motivation becomes of key importance to shape the pattern of economic growth when work is employed in the public sector.[15] This is due to two main reasons. First, the pressure to improve the product in the public sector cannot normally come from market competition, as in the case of the private sector. Intrinsic motivation can take on the role of competition, thus reducing the temptation to rent seeking. Second, the attachment of civil servants to public interest as intrinsically motivated (also called 'public service motivation') can become a model of civic behaviour for all, being under the observation of all citizens as end users of public services.[16] These two reasons must be all the more valid, the greater the provision of the public services necessary to give priority to human development must be.

Finally, if people and governments take human development as the priority in their choices and policies, they must assume an 'ecological morale' and consequent pro-environmental actions. Indeed, the natural environment provides essential inputs to human development, both directly, from energy to beauty, and through social interaction, as it is a public good. The erosion and degradation of the environment, as well as the threat of natural disasters are thus obstacles to human development. Pro-environmental actions are necessary to remove them, thus appearing spontaneous and even enjoyable because linked to motivation for human development (Schmitt et al. 2018; Binder & Blankenberg 2017; Welsch & Kuehling 2017; Pugno & Sarracino 2021). A consequence is that pro-environmental policies may not rely on sanctions or incentives and can take costly actions without becoming unpopular.[17]

In conclusion, the pursuit of human development could change the pattern of economic growth without necessarily turning it into stagnation or de-growth (Pugno 2019). Cyclical instability could be lower and with less damaging effects because of a larger public sector and active macro-economic policies. The rate of long-run growth could benefit from more trustful economic agents, more state-funded basic innovations, and a more efficient public sector. Employment could benefit from more enterprising labour force in finding jobs and even creating new jobs. Consumption goods and services could be more respectful of the environment and of the working conditions because of more responsible consumer behaviours, more volunteer work, and more active pro-environmental policies. Inequalities could be lower because of more equalised opportunities and extended care. Economic growth could thus be even a better proxy for population's well-being.

Making human development a priority in advanced countries, where it is far from being ensured by economic growth, can also help less advanced countries. These, in fact, follow a path of development that is conditioned by the advanced countries through the globalisation of markets, and in particular through the globalisation of consumption patterns and lifestyles. The most striking case is China, which has exhibited extraordinary rates of economic growth in recent decades, yet the trend of subjective well-being of Chinese seems to have declined, thus following the United States (Easterlin et al. 2012).

Making human development a priority over economic growth should be a universal rule, even in cases in which it is costly, such as when facing a pandemic or defending peace. In the long run, everyone will benefit.

Notes

1 Saadi Sedik & Yoo (2021) show that on the basis of past experience, the pandemic accelerates robotisation and automation in production processes, thus displacing low-skilled workers and increasing inequality. Lee et al. (2021) and Garrote Sanchez et al. (2020) provide a first analysis of the sectors and jobs most

vulnerable to pandemic in the US and Europe respectively. Osberg (2021) discusses the consequent increase in economic insecurity. Agostinelli et al. (2020) and Bonacini & Murat (2020) analyse how educational inequality in the US and Europe will increase because of remote learning as a necessary measure against the pandemic.

2 See Alzueta et al. (2020), who adopt a multiple-item self-rating scale of depression and anxiety symptoms over the past 2 weeks; Fiorenzato et al. (2021), who adopt similar scales; and Daly et al. (2020), who adopt the 12-item General Health Questionnaire.

3 Brosig (2002) shows with experiments that face-to-face interaction improves cooperation.

4 Mazzucato (2011) specifies how the state should have a leading and entrepreneurial role in achieving innovation-led growth.

5 The growth trend is higher when recessions are mild rather than when expansions are rapid – Broadberry & Wallis (2016) observe by considering a large number of countries and historical periods.

6 A sample of authoritative commentators of this famous essay is included in the edited book Pecchi & Piga (2008). For a critical discussion of how Keynes has been interpreted, see Pugno (2016a:Ch.7).

7 Psychological studies in the field and in the lab show that having more discretionary time not spent in social or productive activities translates into less well-being (Sharif et al. 2021).

8 In theorising the economics of the family, Nobel laureate Gary Becker treated children as an asset to their parents, so that parents both plan their fertility and invest in children to maximise intergenerational consumption (Becker & Barro 1988).

9 To show that everyone can be creative, a recent experimental study administered a placebo to randomly selected people presenting it as a means to increase creativity. The study observed that participants actually increased their creativity, measured with a computer fantasy game (Rozenkrantz et al. 2017). Another experiment showed that it is possible to induce to make a simple innovation with the same effectiveness both a group that considered themselves creative (engineering and computer science students) and a second group of other students who did not consider themselves creative (Graff Zivi & Lyons 2018).

10 A similar programme to Montessori's is the Reggio approach to primary care, which has been imitated by other schools around Reggio Emilia (Italy) because of its success, as recognised by Heckman and others (Biroli et al. 2017). Recommendations for a more 'creative' school are written in the Report to the UK government by the well-known educator Ken Robinson and his team (Robinson et al. 1999).

11 See Weisleder & Fernald (2013), Romeo et al. (2018), and Lederer et al. (2021) for the need that parents relate to their child by talking and listening to her/him when they spend time together rather than simply looking after her/his safety. According to these studies, the greater the number of words that the parents address directly to their young child, the faster her/his verbal development (while controlling for the education and socio-economic status of the parents), whereas the distraction of a smartphone when they take care of the child proves to be deleterious.

12 For a more detailed discussion on how human development can weaken, see Chapter 3. For evidence on the deleterious consequences on people's well-being of advertising, see Michel et al. (2019).

13   For a discussion on the advantages and limitations of public enterprises relative to private business, with special attention to the knowledge-based sector, see Castelnuovo & Florio (2020).
14   Extrinsic motivation at work arises when the expected reward is economic, being work as painful.
15   Pugno (2006) proves that efficient public services could increase the economy's rate of growth and make it endogenous.
16   According to Ritz et al. (2016), empirical studies on this topic suggest that public service motivation tends to be positively correlated not only with individual and organisational performance but also with job satisfaction and the choice of a job in the public sector. Ayaita et al. (2017) further reveal that public sector employment positively relates to civic virtue even more strongly than to altruism.
17   For the drawbacks of financial sanctions and incentive to steer individuals' pro-environmental actions, see Kirakozian (2016) and Bolderdijk & Steg (2015).

References

Agostinelli F, Doepke M, Sorrenti G, Zilibotti F (2020) When the great equalizer shuts down. *NBER Working Paper*, No. 28264. Cambridge, MA, https://www.nber.org/papers/w28264

Algan Y, Cahuc P (2014) Trust, growth and well-being. In P Aghion, S Durlauf (eds) *Handbook of Economic Growth*. Elsevier, Amsterdam, pp. 49–120

Algan Y, Cahuc P, Shleifer A (2013) Teaching practices and social capital. *American Economic Review: Applied Economics* 5(3):189–210

Allcott H, Braghieri L, Eichmeyer S, Gentzkow M (2020) The welfare effects of social media. *American Economic Review* 110(3):629–676

Altindag DT, Filiz ES, Tekin E (2021) Is online education working? *NBER Working Paper*, No. 29113. Cambridge, MA, https://www.nber.org/papers/w29113

Alzueta E, Perrin P, Baker FC, Caffarra S, Ramos-Usaga D, et al. (2020) How the COVID-19 pandemic has changed our lives. *Journal of Clinical Psychology* 77(3):556–570

Amabile TM, Barsade SG, Mueller JS, Staw BM (2005) Affect and creativity at work. *Administrative Science Quarterly* 50(3):367–403

Amabile T (1998) How to kill creativity. *Harvard Business Review* September:77–87

Anderson N, Potocnik K, Zhou J (2013) Innovation and creativity in organizations. *Journal of Management* 40(5):1297–1333

Andlin-Sobocki P, Jönsson B, Wittchen H-U, Olesen J (2005) Costs of disorders of the brain in Europe. *European Journal of Neurology* 12(1):1–27

Attanasi G, Chess M, Gil-Gallen S, Llerena P (2021). A survey on experimental elicitation of creativity in economics. *Revue d'Economie Industrielle* 174:273–324

Ayaita OA, Gülal F, Yang P (2017) Where does the good shepherd go? *SOEPapers on Multidisciplinary Panel Data Research*, No. 930. Deutsches Institut für Wirtschaftsforschung (DIW), Berlin

Azevedo JP, Hasan A, Goldemberg D, Geven K, Iqbal AS (2021) Simulating the potential impacts of COVID-19 school closures on schooling and learning outcomes. *World Bank Research Observer* 36(1):2–59

Barrett P, Chen S (2021) Social repercussions of pandemics. *IMF Working Paper*, No. 21/21, https://www.imf.org/en/Publications/WP/Issues/2021/01/29/Social-Repercussions-of-Pandemics-50041

Becher M, Longuet Marx N, Pons V, Brouard S, et al (2021) COVID-19, government performance, and democracy. *NBER Working Paper*, No. 29514. Cambridge, MA, https://www.nber.org/papers/w29514

Becker GS, Barro RJ (1988) A reformulation of the economic theory of fertility. *Quarterly Journal of Economics* 103:1–25

Beleche T, Ruhter J, Kolbe A, et al. (2021) COVID-19 Vaccine hesitancy. *ASPE Issue Brief*, May 2021, https://aspe.hhs.gov/sites/default/files/private/pdf/265341/aspe-ib-vaccine-hesitancy.pdf

Bell A, Chetty R, Jaravel X et al. (2019) Who becomes an inventor in America? *Quarterly Journal of Economics* 134:647–713

Binder M, Blankenberg A-K (2017) Green lifestyles and subjective well-being. *Journal of Economic Behavior & Organization* 137:304–323

Biroli P, Del Boca D, Heckman JJ, et al. (2017) Evaluation of the Reggio approach to early education. *NBER Working Paper*, No. 23390. Cambridge, MA, https://www.nber.org/papers/w23390

Blessi GT, Grossi E, Sacco PL, Pieretti G, Ferilli G (2014) Cultural participation, relational goods and individual subjective well-being. *Review of Economics & Finance* 14:34–46

Bolderdijk JW, Steg L (2015) Promoting sustainable consumption. In LA Reisch, J Thøgersen (eds) *Handbook of Research on Sustainable Consumption*. Cheltenham: Elgar, pp. 328–342

Borghans L, Lee Duckworth A, Heckman JJ, Bas ter Weel (2008) The economics and psychology of personality traits. *NBER Working Paper*, No. 13810. Cambridge, MA, https://www.nber.org/papers/w13810

Bonacini L, Murat M (2020) Coronavirus pandemic, remote learning and emerging education inequalities. Department of Economics Marco Biagi, *Working Papers*, No. 177, https://iris.unimore.it/retrieve/handle/11380/1211025/305092/0177.pdf

Boyle PA, Barnes LL, Buchman AS, Bennett DA (2009) Purpose in life is associated with mortality among community-dwelling older persons. *Psychosomatic Medicine* 71:574–579

Broadberry S, Wallis J (2016). Growing, shrinking, and long run economic performance. *NBER Working Paper*, No. 23343. Cambridge, MA, https://www.nber.org/papers/w23343

Brosig J (2002) Identifying cooperative behavior. *Journal of Economic Behavior & Organization* 47:275–290

Bryan M, Alita N (2015) Working hours, work identity and subjective wellbeing. *ISER Working Paper Series*, No. 2015–21. University of Essex, https://www.sheffield.ac.uk/polopoly_fs/1.770120!/file/paper_2018002.pdf

Caliendo M, Uhlendorff A (2015) Locus of control and job search strategies. *Review of Economics and Statistics* 97(1):88–103

Caliendo M, Cobb-Clark DA, Seitz H, Uhlendorff A (2020) Locus of control and investment in training. *Journal of Human Resources* 57(June)

Camerer CF, Hogarth RM (1999) The effects of financial incentives in experiments. *Journal of Risk and Uncertainty* 19:7–42

Cassar L, Meier S (2018) Nonmonetary incentives and the implications of work as a source of meaning. *Journal of Economic Perspectives* 32(3):215–238

Castelnovo P, Florio M (2020) Mission-oriented public organizations for knowledge creation. In *Routledge Handbook of State-Owned Enterprises*. Routledge, Abingdon, pp. 587–604

Chattergoon B, Kerr WR (2021) Winner takes all? *NBER Working Paper*, No. 29456. Cambridge, MA, https://www.nber.org/papers/w29456

Coveri A, Cozza C, Guarascio D (2021) Monopoly capitalism in the digital era. *LEM Working Papers Series* 2021/33. Scuola Superiore Sant'Anna, https://www.lem.sssup.it/WPLem/files/2021-33.pdf

Dabla-Norris E, Khan H, Lima F, Sollaci A (2021) Who doesn't want to be vaccinated? COVID-19. *IMF Working Paper*, No. 21/130, https://www.imf.org/en/Publications/WP/Issues/2021/05/06/Who-Doesnt-Want-to-be-Vaccinated-Determinants-of-Vaccine-Hesitancy-During-COVID-19-50244

Daly M, Sutin AR, Robinson E (2020) Longitudinal changes in mental health and the COVID-19 pandemic. *Psychological Medicine*:1–10

Deming DJ (2017) The growing importance of social skills in the labor market. *Quarterly Journal of Economics* 132(4):1593–1640

Donnelly R, Patrinos HA (2021) Learning loss during COVID-19. *Covid Economics* 77:145–153

Dosi G, Virgillito ME (2019). Whither the evolution of the contemporary social fabric? *International Labour Review* 158(4):594–625

Druckman JN, Klar S, Krupnikov Y, et al. (2021) Affective polarization, local context and public opinion in America. *Nature Human Behavior* 5:28–38

Engzell P, Frey A, Verhaen MD (2021) Learning loss due to school closures during the COVID-19 pandemic. *PNAS* 118(17):e2022376118

D'Orlando F, Ferrante F, Ruiu G (2011) Culturally-based beliefs and labour market institutions. *Journal of Socio-Economics* 40:150–162

Easterlin RA, Morgan R, Switek M, Wang F (2012) China's life satisfaction, 1990–2010. *Proceedings of the National Academy of Sciences* 109(25):9775–9780

Fiorenzato E, Zabberoni S, Costa A, Cona G (2021) Cognitive and mental health changes and their vulnerability factors related to COVID-19 lockdown in Italy. *PLoS ONE* 16(1):e0246204

García JL, Heckman JJ, Leaf DE, Prados MJ (2016) The life-cycle benefits of an influential early childhood program. *NBER Working Paper*, No. 22993. Cambridge, MA, https://www.nber.org/papers/w22993

Garrote SD, Gomez Parra N, Ozden C, Rijkers B (2020) Which jobs are most vulnerable to COVID-19? *Research and Policy Brief*, No. 34. World Bank, Washington, DC

Graff Zivi J, Lyons E (2018) Can innovators be created? *NBER Working Paper*, No. 24339. Cambridge, MA, https://www.nber.org/papers/w24339

Grewenig E, Lergetporer P, Werner K, Woessmann L, Zierow L (2020) COVID-19 and educational inequality. *IZA Discussion Papers*, No. 13820, https://docs.iza.org/dp13820.pdf

Heckman JJ (2008) School, skills, and synapses. *Economic Inquiry* 46(3):289–324

Heckman JJ, Stixrud J, Urzua S (2006) The effects of cognitive and noncognitive abilities on labour market outcomes and social behaviour. *Journal of Labour Economics* 24(3):411–482

Högberg B, Petersen S, Strandh M, et al. (2018) Determinants of declining school belonging 2000–2018. *Social Indicators Research* 157:783–802

Hsieh C-T, Hurst E, Jones CI, Klenow PJ (2019). The allocation of talent and U.S. economic growth. *Econometrica* 87(5):1439–1474

Kahane LH (2021) Politicizing the mask. *Eastern Economic Journal* 47:163–183

Kenney M, Zysman J (2016) The rise of the platform economy. *Issues in Science and Technology* 32(3):61–69

Kerr SP, Kerr WR, Xu T (2017) Personality traits of entrepreneurs. *NBER Working Paper*, No. 24097. Cambridge, MA, https://www.nber.org/papers/w24097

Keynes JM (1930) Economic possibilities for our grandchildren. In *Essays in Persuasion*. New York: W.W. Norton & Co., 1963, pp. 358–373

Khlystova O, Kalyuzhnova Y, Belitski M (2021) The impact of the COVID-19 pandemic on the creative industries. *Journal of Business Research* 139:1192–1210

Kirakozian A (2016) Household waste recycling. *GREDEG Working Papers*, No. 015–09. Université Côte d'Azur, France

Krekel C, Ward G, De Neve J-E (2019) Employee wellbeing, productivity, and firm performance. *Saïd Business School Working Papers* 2019–04, https://papers.ssrn.com/sol3/papers.cfm?abstract_id=3356581

Kurjono K (2018) The entrepreneurial motivation trought locus of control and social interaction. *Advances in Economics, Business and Management Research* 65:17–20

Kuvaas B (2018) The relative efficiency of extrinsic and intrinsic motivation. In A Sasson (ed) *At the Forefront, Looking Ahead*. Universitetsforlaget, Oslo, pp. 198–213

Lackner M, Sunde U, Winter-Ebmer R (2021) COVID-19 and the forces behind social unrest. *CEPR Discussion Paper*, No. DP16756, https://docs.iza.org/dp14884.pdf

Lancet (2021) Editorial. Vol 398 September 18, 2021

Lawton RN, Gramatki I, Watt W, et al. (2020) Does volunteering make us happier, or are happier people more likely to volunteer? *Journal of Happiness Studies* 22:599–624

Lederer Y, Artzi H, Borodkin K (2021) The effects of maternal smartphone use on mother – child interaction. *Child Development*, early view 22 November 2021

Lee SY, Park M, Shin Y (2021) Hit harder, recover slower? *NBER Working Paper*, No. 28354. Cambridge, MA, https://www.nber.org/papers/w28354

Lillard A, Else-Quest N (2006) Evaluating Montessori education. *Science* 313:1893–1894

Lu R, Sheng Y (2020) From fear to hate. *Covid Economics* 39:72–108

Mazzucato (2011) *The Entrepreneurial State*. London: Demos

Michel C, Sovinsky M, Proto E, Oswald AJ (2019) Advertising as a major source of human dissatisfaction. In M Rojas (ed) *The Economics of Happiness*. Springer, Cham, Switzerland, pp. 217–240

Mulligan CB (2020) Deaths of despair and the incidence of excess mortality in 2020. *NBER Working Paper*, No. 28303. Cambridge, MA, https://www.nber.org/papers/w28303

Muringani M, Fitjar RD, Rodriguez-Pose A (2021) Social capital and economic growth in the regions of Europe. *EPA: Economy and Space* 53(6):1412–1434

Nikolova M, Femke C (2020) What makes work meaningful and why economists should care about it. *IZA Discussion Papers*, No. 13112, https://docs.iza.org/dp13112.pdf

OECD (2017) *PISA 2015 Results (Volume III): Students' Well-Being*. Paris: OECD Publishing

OECD (2021) *Tackling the Mental Health Impact of the COVID-19 Crisis*. Paris: OECD Publishing

Osberg L (2021) Economic insecurity and well-being. *DESA Working Paper*, No. 173. ST/ESA/2021/DWP/173, https://desapublications.un.org/working-papers/economic-insecurity-and-well-being

Pecchi L, Piga G (eds) (2008) *Revisiting Keynes*. Cambridge, MA: MIT Press

Phalippou L, Wu BHT (2021) *Brexit & COVID-19 Death Rates*. Retrieved [25 Feb. 2022] from: https://ssrn.com/abstract=3955345

Pickup M, de Rooij E, van der Linden C, Goodwin MJ (2021) Brexit, COVID-19 and attitudes towards immigration in Britain. *Social Science Quarterly* 102(5):2184–2193

Piketty T, Saez E (2013) A theory of optimal taxation. *Econometrica* 81(5):1851–1886

Pugno M (2006) The service paradox and endogenous economic growth. *Structural Change and Economic Dynamics* 17:99–115

Pugno M (2016a) *On the Foundations of Happiness in Economics*. London: Routledge

Pugno M (2016b) Why policies for children, early education and culture? In E Bilancini, L Bruni, PL Porta (eds) *Policies for Happiness*. Oxford: Oxford University Press, pp. 215–238

Pugno M (2019) Happiness, human development, and economic (de)growth. *Annals of the Fondazione Luigi Einaudi* 53:151–172

Pugno M, Depedri S (2010) Job performance and job satisfaction. *Economia Politica-Journal of Analytical and Institutional Economics* 26(1):175–210

Pugno M, Sarracino F (2021) Intrinsic vs extrinsic motivation to protect the environment. *MPRA Paper*, No. 107143, https://mpra.ub.uni-muenchen.de/107143/1/MPRA_paper_107143.pdf

Queadan F, Mensah NA, Tingey B, et al. (2021) The association between opioids, environmental, demographic, and socioeconomic indicators and COVID-19 mortality rates in the United States. *Archives of Public Health* 79:101

Ritz A, Brewer GA, Neumann O (2016) Public service motivation. *Public Administration Review* 76(3):414–426

Robinson K, Minkin L, et al. (1999) *All Our Futures*. London: Department for Education and Employment

Romeo RR, Leonard JA, Robinson ST, et al. (2018) Beyond the 30-million-word gap. *Psychological Science*:1–11

Rozenkrantz L, Mayo AE, Ilan T, Hart Y, et al. (2017) Placebo can enhance creativity. *PLoS ONE* 12(9):e0182466

Saadi Sedik TS, Yoo J (2021) Pandemics and automation. *IMF Working Paper*, No. 21/11, https://www.imf.org/en/Publications/WP/Issues/2021/01/15/Pandemics-and-Automation-Will-the-Lost-Jobs-Come-Back-50000

Schmitt MT, Aknin LB, Axsen J, Shwom RL (2018) Unpacking the relationships between pro-environmental behavior, life satisfaction, and perceived ecological threat. *Ecological Economics* 143:130–140

Sharif MA, Hershfield HE (2021) Having too little or too much time is linked to lower subjective well-being. *Journal of Personality and Social Psychology* 121(4):933–947

Swendsen J (2020) COVID-19 and mental health: how one pandemic can reveal another. *Journal of Behavioral and Cognitive Therapy* 30:161–163

Trautmann S, Rehm J, Wittchen H (2016) The economic costs of mental disorders. *EMBO Reports* 17(9):1245–1249

Valero A, Riom C, Oliveira-Cunha J (2021) The business response to Covid-19 one year on. *Centre for Economic Performance*, No. 024, https://cep.lse.ac.uk/pubs/download/cepcovid-19-024.pdf

van der Ploeg F (2006) The making of cultural policy. In V Ginsburgh, D Throsby (eds) *Handbook of the Economics of Art and Culture*. Amsterdam: North-Holland, pp. 1183–1221

Weibel A, Katja R, Weibel A (2007) *Crowding-out of Motivation. Arbeitspapier der Universität Zürich und Social Science Research Network*. Retrieved [25 Feb. 2022] from: http://papers.ssrn.com/sol3/papers.cfm?abstract_id=957770

Weisleder A, Fernald A (2013) Talking to children matters. *Psychological Science* 24:2143–2152

Welsch H, Kuehling J (2017) How green self image affects subjective well-being. *Oldenburg Discussion Papers in Economics*, No. 404, https://www.econstor.eu/bitstream/10419/171170/1/V-404-17.pdf

Wittchen HU, Jacobi F, Rehm J, et al. (2015) The size and burden of mental disorders and other disorders of the brain in Europe 2010. *European Neuropsychopharmacology* 21:655–679

Zuboff S (2019) Surveillance capitalism and the challenge of collective action. *New Labor Forum* 28(1):10–29

Epilogue

John Maynard Senyek awoke one morning from a restless sleep. The evening before, he had stayed up late for a report that he had to prepare for the opening of the academic year 2030/2031. The report was to illustrate the cyclical economic phase that was looming weak. He wanted to reassure markets and businesses by arguing that only minor policy adjustments were needed to gradually bring the economy back to the usual growth path after years of global pandemic, environmental disasters, and even wars. However, Senyek was not satisfied with the report and continued to polish it until he collapsed from sleep.

On that night, the audience he imagined focused on his words and lit up by press flashes became, in his dream, a noisy crowd of surprised and annoyed faces. And the adorned lecture hall became a bare room that resounded with the words that arrived sharply from the stage.

"In a hundred years, the entire economy will slow down to settle into secular stagnation. The technology will advance amazingly, but the great mass of citizens will not feel richer. Many will find to work, but the normal work will be on call for a few hours throughout the day and night, at the screen or on the street. Yet, thanks to technology, all people will be able to immerse themselves in their preferred virtual life between one work call and the next. They will thus be able to enjoy on command and escape the worries of real life. They will no longer have to think about their future, about the dangers for the peoples of the earth. Technology will provide everyone with the possibility of an adventurous or restful, heroic or social life but still a virtual one. People will eventually live in such a symbiosis with machines that their original humanity will be lost without too much awareness in a slow metamorphosis".

As Seynek recovered from the shock, he realised that he had to react. He stood up rapidly, tore up his report, and wrote in a few points all that was necessary for that nightmare to remain so forever. He knew what risks he would run for his career; he knew how utopian his recommendations

DOI: 10.4324/9781003241676-7

were. But with the new report, he intended to voice an urgency that could no longer be hidden. First, to drop the priority given to economic growth that made people's lives a continuous search for comfort and even a virtual existence. Second, to build the conditions that would enable each person to live every minute, easy or difficult, to develop those capabilities to imagine and to collaborate with others for a future of overall human development. As Keynes wished for one hundred years before, everyone had to know how to "cultivate the art of life", a premise for an enduring well-being. But to this end, it is necessary from now on to prepare the conditions for peace and social cohesion and to govern the demographic dynamics, the direction of science and of economic growth.

Index

addiction 4, 30, 34, 55, *56*, 61, 64, 72–76, 97; as a choice 73–74, 77n30; and high-tech products 61, 62, 73–75
advanced countries or advanced economies 3, 8, 12, 13, 57, 58, 70, 74, 91
aspirations 4, 15, 30, 58, 91; for consumption 73
attachment, psychology of 41, 73, 77n31

Baumol, William 4, 66, 70, 76n6, 79, 86, 96
Becker, Gary 44, 47n10, 49, 72, 76n10, 79, 103n8, 105
Brexit: and hate crimes 21; vote for 19
Bush, George H.W. 10

Canada 21n1, 21n7, 57, 58
capabilities: and the capability approach 3, 32; *see also* creativity-and-sociality
China 10, 19, 20, 21, 89, 102
comparison with others 35, 45, 58, 64, 76n2, 98
concentration of production 10, 57, 88, 96, 97
consumerism 4, *56*, 60, 61; *see also* materialism
COVID-19 pandemic 1, 4, 10, 11, 28, 30; hindrance for human development 87–90; opportunity for human development 90–91
creativity *see* creativity-and-sociality
creativity-and-sociality: as distinctively human 3, 34–35; evolutionary origin of 3, 35–37; as fundamental human capability 33–34; internality and externality of 34, 39; origin and development from birth of 37–38; *see also* human development, the fundamental
culture *or* cultural activities *or* cultural services 35, 37, 48n22, 62, 66, 70, 88, 96, 99, 100
cyclical instability 4, 55, *56*, 57, 59, 60, 62, 76n3, 87, 97, 102

depression: economic 5, 10; mental 18, 22n21; *see also* ill-being

Easterlin, Richard x, 12, 13, 16, 24, 25, 26, 45, 50, 53, 102, 106; the paradox of 13, 16
economic growth: changed pattern of 99–102; deceleration of 8–11; its inability to predict well-being 2, 3, 11–13; in Italy 14–15; in the US 16, 28
'economic problem' 2, 3, 5
education 40, 64–68, 70–72, 76n12, 77, 88, 92; and the labour market 62; policy for 93–96, 99, 100; in UNDP 28, 29, 32; *see also* parenting
environment: behaviour in favour of 34, 44, 46n4, 102; the degradation of 1, 28, 33, 55, 56, *56*, 60, 61, 91; policy for 31, 60–61, 75, 91, 96, 99, 100, 102, 104n17
environmental approach 28, 29, 31, 34; strengths and weaknesses of 31
environmental sustainability 2, 4

eudaimonia 41; measures of 31
European countries: and addiction 74;
economic insecurity in 77n16; food
waste in 76n8; growth of 11; income
comparison in 76n2; inequality in
58, 76n5; and the labour market 63,
76n13, 76n14, 76n15; mental health
expenditure in 93; and the pandemic
103n1; populism and nationalism
in 29, 30; similarities with the US
16, 29; well-being trend of 12, 13,
14–15, 22n9, 22n10, 59, 65
extrinsic motivation 39, 42, 47n13,
76n7, 101, 104n14

GDP, movement going beyond 2, 3,
28–32; growth of (*see* economic
growth)
Germany 8, 9, 13, 16, 19, 21n7,
22n976n13, 77n14, 77n16
globalisation 8, 10, 57, 76n12, 102
Great Recession of 2008–2009 1, 15,
18, 57, 62, 83, 87

happiness 1, 2, 3, 12, 16, 18, 21, 22n15,
23n21, 28, 30, 31, 41, 42; *see also*
well-being
Heckman, James x, 46n7, 48, 51,
69–71, 73, 82, 83, 99, 100, 103n10,
105, 106
high-tech consumption 4, *56*, 62, 88,
97; addiction to 74, 75
Homo economicus 4, 43–44
Homo sociologicus 4, 44–45
human development, the
fundamental: definition of 2–4,
32–34; and economic deprivations
92; explanation of the weakening
of 60; and the fundamental human
capability 32; going beyond the
Capability Approach 32; and
health policy 93; and ill-being
43–46; as an input-ouput process
39–40; the maximisation of 40;
the need for time for 59–60; the
self-generating property of 34,
38–40; strategy to prioritising 91;
and uncertainty 39, 47n15, 60;
and well-being 41–43; *see also*
creativity-and-sociality

ill-being 3, 17, 43, 44, 58, 73, 74, 76n7,
93; *see also* depression, mental
inequality 4, 55, *56*, 57–60, 76n3, 76n5,
87, 92, 97, 98, 102n1, 103n1
insecurity 4, *56*, 57, 59, 63, 64, 87,
88, 98
intrinsic motivation 39, 40, 42, 43,
47n13, 47n14, 47n19, 100, 101
Italy 8, *9*, 13, 14–15, 19, 21n7, 22n9,
74, 89, 103n10

Japan 8, *9*, 13, 15, 16, 21n7

Keynes, John Maynard: and the 'art
of life' 6, 111; and the 'economic
problem' 3, 5; his 1930 speech 1,
3, 5, 77n18, 83, 93, 103n6, 107; the
three predictions 2–3, 5–6; and the
'well-being problem' 3, 5

life satisfaction: the approach of 30;
the questionnaire question 12; the
weaknesses of 30–31
locus of control 45, 68, 71, 76n7,
77n28, 100

Maslow, Abraham 67, 76n1
materialism 60, 76n7; *see also*
consumerism
mobility, economic 58
motivation *see* extrinsic motivation;
intrinsic motivation

nationalism 19, 20, 99
Nussbaum, Martha 32, 46n1

Obama, Barack 10
opioids, use of 74, 84

parenting 4, 37, 40, 55, 67, 68–72, 76,
94, 103n8, 103n11; styles 69, 71
personality traits and fundamental
human development 40–41
platforms system 97; and the labour
market 98; and producers' pressure
98; public 98; regulation of 99
policies: to prioritise human
development 91–99; to revive
growth 3, 8–10
populism 19, 23n22, 89

rationality and creativity 45–46

Scitovsky, Tibor x, 26, 47n13, 47n17, 53
Sen, Amartya ix, 32, 46n1, 48n29
social cohesion: deterioration of 18–21
sociality *see* creativity-and-sociality
suicides: in the US 15, 17, 88;
    see also ill-being

technical progress 5, 8, 11, *56*, 56, 59,
    66, 68, 70, 76n12; and the impact on
    the labour market 57, 62, 64
technology: the turn from useful to
    pleasant 61; *see also* high-tech
    consumption; technical progress
Thatcher, Margaret 8
time: and education 56, 59, 60, 66, 69,
    70, 71, 77nn24–25, 103n11; essential
    in fundamental human development
    39–40, 47n16; free 4, 5, 75, 94, 95,
    96; and high-tech consumption 75,
    76, 88; as an input 39, 40, 44, 57, 92,
    93, 95, 96; learning 33, 43, 47n16,
    62, 88; leisure 39, 62, 65; 59, 60;
    shift in the use of 65; and technology
    61; working 4, 5, 59, 61, 62, 65, 95
Trump Donald: and the deterioration
    of social cohesion 20; the election
    of 19; and hate crimes 20; and the
    opioid crisis 74
trust in others *or* general trust 20, 21,
    22, 58, 68, 75, 76n5, 90, 100, 101,
    102

uncertainty 8, 11, 31, 39, 47n15, 60, 70, 92
unemployment 5, 10, 18, 57, 62–64, 88,
    92, 101; technological 101

United Kingdom 5, 8, *9*, 88, 13, 15, 16,
    20, 21, 21n7, 22n9, 22n21, 23n25,
    76n13, 77n14, 77n16, 77n27, 88, 89,
    103n10
United Nations Development
    Program: strengths and
    weaknesses of 29–30
United States: addiction in the
    74, 78n33, 98; and the 'death
    of despair' 15, 88; declining
    well-being in 3, 4, 7–8, 13,
    15–18, 28, 55, 58–59, 75, 102;
    and deteriorating social cohesion
    45; economic insecurity in the 57,
    62, 63, 103n1; education in the
    66–68, 69, 71, 77n24, 77n25; and
    environmental degradation 61;
    growth of the 7–11, 21, 57; income
    comparison in the 76n2, 76n5;
    inequality in the 57–58; and the
    labour market 61, 62–64; the opioid
    crisis in the 74; and populism and
    nationalism 19–20, 89–90; and time
    use 65, 75; the use of high-tech
    products in the 75

well-being: explanation of the decline
    of 55–62; and fundamental human
    development 41–43; Italy's decline
    of 14–15; Japan's decline of 13;
    measured as subjective 12; the two
    pathways to 42–43; problem 2, 3,
    5, 6; UK's decline of 13, 22n21;
    US's decline of 15–18; as usually
    predicted by economic growth 7,
    28, 41; *see also* happiness;
    ill-being